Collins

THE TIMES
SPELLING
BEE

Spell like a champion

HarperCollins Publishers
Westerhill Road
Bishopbriggs
Glasgow
G64 2QT

First edition 2009

Reprint 10 9 8 7 6 5 4 3 2 1 0

© HarperCollins Publishers 2009

ISBN 978-0-00-731841-4

Collins ® is a registered trademark of
HarperCollins Publishers Limited

The Times is a registered trademark of
Times Newspapers Limited

All rights in the "Lexi" character and
image are owned by Times Newspapers
Limited

Puzzles © James David 2009

www.collinslanguage.com
www.timesspellingbee.com

A catalogue record for this book is
available from the British Library

Typeset by Wordcraft, Glasgow

Printed in Great Britain by Clays Ltd,
St Ives plc

Acknowledgements
We would like to thank those authors
and publishers who kindly gave
permission for copyright material to be
used in the Collins Word Web. We would
also like to thank Times Newspapers Ltd
for providing valuable data.

Contents

EDITORIAL STAFF
Helen Hucker
Elspeth Summers

FOR THE PUBLISHER
Lucy Cooper
Elaine Higgleton

TEACHER CONSULTANTS
Amanda Alexander, Lex Education
Rachel Gee, Lex Education

PUZZLE COMPILER
James David

INTRODUCTION
Why is Spelling Important?

The main reason spelling is important is communication. Communication is a two-way process – understanding others and making yourself understood.

Understanding other people

If you are a confident speller, you will be able to read and understand written material easily and efficiently. Reading will probably be more fun, so you will read more. As a result, your reading, spelling and writing are likely to improve.

Making yourself understood

If your writing is full of spelling mistakes, other people may find it hard to understand what you are trying to say. If a word is spelled incorrectly, they may struggle to work out which word you meant. If you are trying to persuade them to take your side in an argument, it may be more difficult to convince them. Poor spelling reduces the appeal and effectiveness of written work.

The spelling debate

Do you think that your school is wasting your time teaching you how to spell? Do you think that it's fine as

long as your text messages can be read and your webchats can be understood? Do you think time spent learning spellings could be better used learning more interesting things? You are not alone. This has been much debated.

In 2008 a well-known British academic claimed that schools put too much emphasis on teaching spelling and that the time would be spent more usefully teaching other subjects. He suggested that pupils should be allowed to spell words in ways that appeared logical. Unsurprisingly, suggestions like this provoke strong reactions both for and against.

Some people argue passionately to keep English spelling as it is. Others argue, equally passionately, that the English language should move with the times. They say we should allow spellings to change according to how words are *often* spelled, rather than how they *ought to be* spelled.

Spelling reform is a controversial subject. The reformers argue that simplifying English spelling would give teachers more time to teach other, more valuable subjects. Pupils would be more confident and able readers and writers, and this improved literacy would have a positive effect on all areas of the curriculum. Young people would leave school with a better education and all society would benefit from this potential workforce of literate and confident achievers.

However, spelling reform is not something that happens quickly or cheaply. The reform of German spelling that was introduced formally in August 1998 was the result of almost 20 years of debate, including legal challenges and court cases against its introduction. The introduction was followed by a 'transition phase' of seven years. It is clear that, if the English spelling system were to be reformed, it would not be a quick process. If the German example is anything to go by, a quarter of a century is not an unreasonable estimate of how long it would take to bring it about.

It is clear, therefore, that English spelling is not going to change any time soon.

Spellcheckers - friend or foe?

Nowadays, most people do the bulk of their writing (for example, essays, reports and letters) on a computer. All word-processing packages have built-in spellcheckers.

These can be a bit of mixed blessing. They are useful for highlighting and correcting simple typing errors, such as an extra letter (for example, **greeen** instead of **green**) or letters in the wrong order (for example, **teh** instead of **the**). Spellcheckers do have their drawbacks and it is not a good idea to rely totally on one to find any errors in your written work.

The potential problems with spellcheckers are:

American English v British English

There are a number of spelling differences between these two varieties of English. British English has **labour**, **licence** (the noun), **centre**, **labelled** and **tyre**, while American English has **labor**, **license**, **center**, **labeled** and **tire**. Sometimes verb parts are different, as in the past tense of **dive** - **dived** in British English and **dove** in American. This is a problem for British users of American spellcheckers, which will automatically 'correct' a British spelling to its American equivalent.

Homophones

A homophone is a word that sounds the same as another word but is spelled differently and has a different meaning; for example, **write** and **right** or **hair** and **hare**. If you were to type *The fox was chasing the hair across the field* the spellchecker would not pick up the misspelling. **Hair** and **hare** are both accepted nouns and a spellchecker has no way of knowing which is correct in that sentence. So the error goes unnoticed.

Spellcheckers can get it wrong too

A spellchecker is only as good as the word list that was used to create it. If the list has mistakes and omissions, the spellchecker will highlight correctly spelled words as being incorrect. A few years ago the spellchecker in a well-known word-processing package had a mistake. The word **liaison** had been incorrectly included as 'liason', without the second 'i'. So the spellchecker showed the correct spelling as wrong, and suggested an incorrect spelling as a replacement.

While a spellchecker is a useful tool, you should never rely on it to do the whole job of checking a piece of text. You should read what you have written and check any words you are not sure about in a good dictionary. If you always have trouble with certain words (and even the best spellers do), pay particular attention to them when you are reading over your work. If you can, ask someone else to read it as well. There's no shame in getting your work checked.

Above all, remember that it is worth the extra time and effort to get it right.

A thought to the future

It seems like a long way off, but in a few years' time you might be applying for a college place or a job. And when you write your application letter or your CV, you'll want to be sure your spellings are all correct. By learning your spellings now, you'll be safe in the knowledge that you are creating the right impression with a prospective tutor or employer.

Although some people believe that spelling is not important and are not put off by mistakes in a piece of writing, it is safe to assume that an equal (or possibly greater) number think that spelling does matter, and that poor spelling is an indication of other failings.

Many employers say that they will not even consider interviewing candidates whose spelling is poor, regardless of their qualifications or experience. They take the view, rightly or wrongly, that an application form or letter with spelling mistakes is a sign that the candidate is one or more of the following:

- poorly educated
- not very intelligent
- not that interested in getting the job – if they were interested they would have taken more care over the application
- sloppy and lazy

These assumptions may be unfair, but employers have the right to reject candidates for jobs on the basis of their application letters or CVs alone. If the first piece of correspondence between you and your prospective employer is full of spelling mistakes, it is unlikely you will get a chance to show them how smart, hard-working and enthusiastic you really are.

In this book, we have tried to include the most common words you are likely to encounter in your reading and writing. However, you may come across words we have left off our lists. If you do, you can use a dictionary to check the spelling and meaning and then add them to the relevant page in this book.

Spell Like a Champion has been researched with teachers to ensure that it includes information from the National Curriculum. This book provides the information on spelling that students need to allow them to improve their performance. It is accessible, student-friendly and relevant to school work in all subjects.

Helen Hucker
Editor
Collins Dictionaries

CHAPTER ONE
Why We Misspell

English is generally considered to be a hard language to spell. Why is that? Well, there are four main reasons.

1. Words that sound the same have different spellings.

These are known as homophones, from Greek *homos* meaning 'same' and *phōnē* meaning 'sound'. There are a large number of these in English and people often get confused about which spelling is correct. For example:

altar **alter**	part of a church to change
break **brake**	to damage to stop a vehicle
coarse **course**	vulgar route
cue **queue**	prompt line of people waiting

dual **duel**	double fight between two people
flair **flare**	talent flame
hoard **horde**	hidden store large crowd
led **lead**	past tense of verb 'lead' metal
licence **license**	certificate giving permission to grant a licence
miner **minor**	person who digs for coal of lesser importance
practice **practise**	repetition of an activity to repeat an activity
principal **principle**	most important and the most important person standard or rule
stationary **stationery**	not moving writing materials
their **they're** **there**	belonging to them short for 'they are' in that place

to	in the direction of
too	as well
two	number between one and three
vain	too proud
vein	blood vessel
your	I like your name
you're	you're good at football

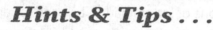

Hints & Tips . . .

With a particular word that is difficult:

- picture it in your head
- make the font really big
- colour the difficult part of the word
- look at it forwards and backwards.

2. The word is not spelled the way it is pronounced.

This happens often in English. This is because some spellings were established and accepted as standard according to the word's pronunciation at that time. But then the pronunciation changed, while the spelling stayed the same, leaving a word that sounds quite different from its spelling.

Old English was originally written in runes before Christian missionaries introduced the Latin or Roman alphabet that we know today.

ᛒ ᚠ ᚱ ᛈ ᚦ ᛐ ↑ ᛗ

The problem with using the Roman alphabet for English spelling was that there were more sounds than there were letters to represent them. This meant that combinations of letters had to be used to represent some of the English sounds, such as 'gh' for the original sound in the middle of the word **night**, which sounded like the sound that Scottish people say at the end of the word **loch**. As there was no Roman equivalent for this, scribes (and later, typesetters) used the letters available to them in the Roman alphabet, and came up with the 'gh' combination that is found so frequently in English words. This problem persists in English today, where there are about 44 phonemes used (and still only 26 letters in the alphabet!).

The history of English pronunciation and borrowing from other languages also accounts for the number of letters that are silent in English words. It is believed that almost all of the 26 letters of the English alphabet are silent in at least one word. Here are some of the more common ones:

a (bread, deaf, head)
b (comb, doubt, limb)
c (indict, muscle, scissors)
d (handsome, sandwich, Wednesday)
e (have, give, love)
g (gnat, phlegm, sign)
h (ghost, honest, rhyme, vehicle)
i (business)
k (knife, knight, know)
l (calm, salmon, talk, would)
m (mnemonic)
n (autumn, condemn, hymn)
o (leopard)
p (psychiatry, receipt)

r (arm, fir, heart, turn) – this is not true of every accent: for example Scottish speakers pronounce the **r** in these words
s (island, viscount)
t (castle, listen, mortgage)
w (sword, two, write)

3. There is more than one way to represent a sound.

The same sounds (or phonemes) can be spelled in a number of ways. It was supposedly George Bernard Shaw who pointed out that, because of the number of ways there are to represent one phoneme in English, **fish** could quite reasonably be written **ghoti** – **gh** sounds like **f** in **tough**; **o** sounds like **i** in **women**; and **ti** sounds like **sh** in **nation**.

The vowel sounds in the following groups of words have the same pronunciation.

march, alms, clerk and heart
act and plait
dive, aisle, guy, might and rye
fire, buyer, liar and tyre

out and crowd
flour and flower
bet, said and says
paid, day, deign, gauge, grey and neigh
bear, dare, prayer, stair and where
fit, build, nymph and sieve
see, siege, mete and pleat
fear, beer, mere and tier
note, beau, dough, hoe and slow
thaw, broad, drawer, fault, halt and ought
void and boy
pull, good and should
zoo, do, queue, shoe, spew, true and you
poor, skewer and sure
fern, burn, fir, learn, term and worm (not in all accents)
cut, flood, rough and son

See page 63 for a list of long vowel sounds.

The consonant sounds in bold in the following groups of words have the same pronunciation.

bank and ru**bb**ed
daisy, re**d**, la**dd**er, coul**d** and **dh**al
fun, to**ff**, cou**gh** and **ph**armacy
goat, mu**gg**y and **gh**ost
kangaroo, **c**andle, **Ch**ristmas, **kh**aki, bri**ck**, tal**k**, s**ch**eme, pu**kk**a and stu**cc**o
leaf, ni**l**, fa**ll**, **ll**ama and koh**l**
make, sli**mm**ed, co**me**, ru**m**, thu**mb** and da**mn**
note, pa**n**, fu**nn**y, to**nn**e, **kn**ife, **gn**ome, **pn**eumonia and **mn**emonic
pretty and ha**pp**y
rat, cu**rr**ent, **rh**yme and **wr**ong
sit, pu**s**, mi**ss**, **ps**ychiatry, **sc**ent and re**c**eive
tip, pa**tt**er, de**bt**, fi**ght** and indi**ct**

van, spi**v**, co**v**er and **W**eimaraner

well and **wh**ite (not in all accents)

zip, fi**zz**, ma**z**e, day**s**, plea**s**e, **ts**ar and **cz**ar

Hints & Tips . . .

Key words you find difficult to spell into a Word document on your computer, save them on your mobile, or buy an address book with alphabet tabs and make your own personalized spelling help book.

The sounds in bold in the following groups of words have the same pronunciation.

shoe, **s**ugar, **ch**ute, ti**ss**ue, na**ti**on, o**ce**an, con**sci**ous, an**xi**ous, man**si**on, spe**ci**al and **sch**edule

trea**s**ure, a**z**ure, clo**s**ure and eva**s**ion

chew and na**t**ure

jaw, adjective, lodge, soldier and usage

books, walks, kicks and mix

4. Many English words have been brought in from other languages.

One of the most striking features of the English language is its readiness to accept words from other languages. This has been going on for centuries. Latin, Greek and Old Norse were early sources of borrowed words, followed by French, which had a huge impact on English after the Norman Conquest. European languages such as Italian, Spanish, German and Dutch have all contributed words to English.

As English speakers spread out from western Europe, they came into contact with languages further afield, and introduced new words from an astonishing range of languages: Arabic, Chinese, Hindi, Russian, Turkish and Persian. The growth of the British Empire meant English speakers were coming into contact with languages all across the world, and this contact is reflected in the words taken in from Sanskrit, Australian Aboriginal languages, Maori, Tamil, Malay and the languages of the Native Canadian peoples. In recent years, words have come in from Japanese, Urdu, Gujarati and Punjabi.

It is this magpie-like tendency to steal from other languages that lends English its vitality. The downside, however, is that it has produced a large body of words that conform to no fixed English spelling pattern. These words can be particularly tricky to spell. You can read more about these borrowed words in the section called 'Where does English spelling come from?'

FAQ . . .

Why is the plural of mouse 'mice', when the plural of 'house' isn't 'hice'? 'Mouse' and 'house' form their plurals in different ways because their plurals differed in their original language. In Old English 'mouse' was *mus* and the plural was *mys*. The plural became 'mice' in English to match the pronunciation. However, the plural of 'house' in Old English was the same as the singular, *hus*, so the plural would have been 'house' as well. Because we like to have our plurals marked in English, we regularized it with the standard –s suffix.

Some Commonly Misspelled Words

a

aardvark	actually	agility
ability	addict	agricultural
able	addiction	agriculture
abroad	addition	alcohol
abscess	address	alkaline
abseil	adieu	alliteration
absorb	adjacent	alphabet
abstract	advertise	alphabetical
accelerate	advertisement	alternate
accommodation	aerate	although
achieve	aeronautical	amateur
achievement	aerosol	ameliorate
acid	aesthetic	amenity
acquire	aficionado	amount
acrylic	aggravate	amphibian
active	aggressive	anaesthesia
activity	agile	anaesthetic

analgesic

analyse

analysis

androgynous

angle

anoint

Antarctic

antediluvian

anthology

apartheid

apartment

apocryphal

apostrophe

appal

appalling

apparatus

apparent

applause

approval

approve

approximately

apropos

aqueduct

arbitrary

archaeology

archetypal

argument

artefact

article

athlete

athletic

atlas

atmosphere

audacious

audible

audience

auspicious

author

authority

autumn

average

axes

axis

b

bachelor

bait

baptism

baroque

beautiful

beginning

beguile

beige

believe

beneath

besiege

bias

biased

Bible

biblical

bicep

binary

bivouac

blasphemous

blatant

bonsai

boudoir

boycott

brief

brioche

broccoli

Buddhism

Buddhist

budget

burgeon

burial

buried

business

byte

Byzantine

C

cable

cacophony

calculate

calendar

camouflage

cappuccino

carbohydrate

Caribbean

cartridge

castle

catalogue

category

caterwaul

cathedral

Catholic

caught

CD-ROM

celebrate

celebration

cemetery

centimetre

ceremony

chagrin

character

characteristic

charcoal

chauffeur

chemical

chocolate

choir

chord

chorus

Christian

chromatic

chronological

chronology

cinnamon

cipher

circulate

circulation

circumference

citizen

civilisation

classification

clause

claustrophobia

cliché

climate

climb

computer

contour

cognac

concentration

contradict

cognoscenti

concessionary

contradiction

coiffure

conciliate

control

collage

conclusion

co-ordinate

collection

condensation

copyright

colonisation

conductor

cornucopia

colony

conflict

corresponding

colour

conjunction

costume

column

connect

country

combustion

connection

county

comma

connoisseur

couture

commandment

conscience

creation

commemorate

conscious

crosshatch

commiserate

consensus

crotchet

commitment

consequence

current

committee

consonant

curriculum

communication

constitution

cursor

comparative

constitutional

curtain

comparison

contemporaneous

cycle

compatible

contemporary

cynicism

component

content

cyst

composition

continuous

d

data

database

daughter

debutante

deceive

decide

decimal

decipher

decision

defence

definite

degree

delete

denominator

denouement

depend

dependency

dependent

desert

desiccate

design

despair

desperate

detach

detente

development

dialogue

dialysis

diameter

diamond

diarrhoea

diary

dictionary

diet

dietetic

digest

digestion

digit

dimension

director

disappear

disappoint

disassemble

disastrous

disciple

discipline

discussion

disease

disk

display

dissatisfied

dissatisfy

diuretic

diurnal

divide

division

document

dramatise

dynamics

dynasty

e

easel

ecclesiastical

economic

economical

economy

ecstasy

editor

effervescent

effete

effort

eighth

electronic

element

emaciate

embarrass

embryo

emigration

emotion

emotional

employment

encourage

encouragement

encyclopaedia

energy

engagement

enquire

ensemble

entente

enthral

entourage

entrance

environment

ephemeral

epistle

equation

equilateral

equipment

erosion

espionage

espresso

estimate

estuary

eulogy

euphemism

euphoria

eureka

euthanasia

evaluation

evaporation

evidence

eviscerate

exacerbate

exaggerate

excellent

excerpt

exchange

exclamation

exercise

exhibition

exhilarate

exist

exit

experience

explanation

expression

extract

extraneous

extraordinary

extraterrestrial

extravagant

extrovert

f

fabric	fierce	fraction
façade	fiery	freeze
facetious	figurative	freight
facile	flour	frequency
faith	flowchart	friction
falsetto	fluorescent	frieze
fantasy	foetus	fulfil
fascinate	foreground	function
February	foreign	funeral
festival	foresee	furore
fibre	forty	furthermore
field	fourth	

g

gallery	generous	gourmet
gambol	genre	government
garrotte	gingham	graffiti
gastronomic	glamorous	grammar
gateau	glamour	graph
gauge	globe	graphic
gender	glossary	growth
generally	gorgeous	guarantee
generosity	gourmand	guard

guardian	guess	gym
guerrilla	guile	gymnastic

h

habitat	hazard	honorary
haemorrhage	health	honour
halcyon	height	horizontal
hallelujah	heinous	humorous
hamster	heredity	humour
hamstring	heterogeneous	hygiene
handkerchief	hierarchy	hymn
happened	hieroglyphic	hyperbole
harass	highlight	hypnotic
hardware	Hindu	hypocrisy
harmony	Hinduism	

i

icon	imagination	imperialism
idiosyncrasy	immediate	impresario
illegible	immigrant	improvise
illusion	immoral	inconsequential
imagery	immorality	independence
imaginary	imperial	independent

index

indict

indispensable

industrial

infrastructure

ingénue

ingredient

injury

innocuous

innovation

inoculate

input

insect

inseparable

insouciant

inspire

instalment

instrument

instrumental

integrate

intelligent

interactive

interesting

interface

international

internet

interrupt

interval

introvert

invasion

involve

involvement

irregular

irrelevance

irrelevant

irritable

Islam

isosceles

Israel

issue

itinerary

j

jamboree

jaundice

jealous

jealousy

jeopardy

jewellery

Jewish

joule

jubilee

Judaism

judgment

judicial

juggernaut

jugular

jurisdiction

justify

juvenile

juxtaposition

k

kaleidoscopic	keyboard	knife
kamikaze	kiln	knight
karaoke	kilogram	knives
kernel	kilometre	knowledge
kerosene	kleptomania	kumquat

l

label	leviathan	listening
laboratory	liaison	litre
labyrinthine	librarian	location
lackadaisical	library	lonely
landscape	lieutenant	longitude
languor	lighting	lovely
latitude	lightning	lugubrious
league	linen	luminescence
leaven	liquefy	lyric
leisure	liquid	

m

macabre	magazine	major
machine	maintenance	malign
maelstrom	maisonette	malleable

mammal

manoeuvre

manufacture

margarine

marriage

masquerade

massacre

material

mathematician

mayonnaise

meanwhile

measure

medicine

medieval

Mediterranean

megabyte

melange

melody

memento

memoir

memory

meretricious

messianic

metamorphosis

metaphor

method

metre

millennium

millionaire

mineral

miniature

minim

minor

minus

minuscule

minutiae

miracle

miscellaneous

mischief

mischievous

misdemeanour

misogynist

misspell

mobile

mobility

moccasin

modem

modern

module

monitor

moral

morality

moreover

mortgage

motive

movement

multimedia

multiplication

multiply

murmur

muscle

musician

Muslim

myriad

myth

n

narrative	negative	nomenclature
narrator	neighbour	non-fiction
nation	nervous	noticeable
national	network	novel
natural	neuralgia	numerator
nauseate	neurosis	nutrient
necessary	niece	nutrition

o

obsequious	omelette	organism
obsess	omit	original
obstreperous	onomatopoeia	output
occasion	opaque	outrageous
occurrence	ophthalmic	oxygen
ochre	opportunity	oxygenate
octave	orchestra	
official	orchestral	

p

palette	paraffin	paralytic
pamphlet	paragraph	paraphernalia
parable	parallel	paraplegic
paradigm	parallelogram	parliament

participation

particle

password

pastel

pattern

peaceful

peccadillo

peculiar

pedagogue

penchant

penitential

people

perceive

percentage

percussion

perform

performance

perimeter

permanent

pernicious

perpendicular

perseverance

persistent

personal

personification

perspective

perspicacious

persuade

persuasion

pharaoh

pharmaceutical

philanthropy

phlegm

photocopy

phraseology

physical

picaresque

piece

pigeon

pilgrim

pilgrimage

piquant

pitch

plagiarize

playwright

plural

poignant

political

politics

pollution

polyester

portfolio

portrait

position

positive

possession

potential

poverty

pray

prayer

precede

predator

prefer

preference

prefix

prejudice

preparation

preposition

prerogative

presentation

pressure

preview

priest

prioritise

privilege

process

processor

production

professor

programme

proletariat

pronunciation

propaganda

prophet

proportion

proposition

protein

Protestant

provincial

provision

psychedelic

psychology

pubescence

publisher

q

quadriceps

quadrilateral

qualify

quaver

query

questionnaire

queue

quintessential

r

racism

racist

raconteur

radius

rapport

rapprochement

ratatouille

ratio

reaction

realignment

reality

rebel

rebellion

receipt

receive

recipe

recommend

reconnaissance

recoup

recurring

reference

reflect

reflection

refrigerator

region

regional

regular

rehearsal
rehearse
reign
relationship
relay
relevance
relevant
relief
religion
religious
remember
rendezvous
represent

representative
reproduce
republic
research
resolution
resources
respiration
respire
restaurant
resuscitate
revolt
revolution
reward

rhetoric
rhinoceros
rhombus
rhyme
rhythm
ricochet
ridiculous
risotto
role
romance
rotate
rotation
rural

S

sabotage
saboteur
sacrilege
safety
sanctimonious
sanction
sandal
satellite
Saturday

sausage
scale
scanner
scenario
scene
schedule
schizophrenic
scissors
score

script
secondary
section
seismic
seize
semibreve
sensible
sensor
separate

sepulchre

sequence

sergeant

series

server

settlement

sew

sexism

sexist

share

shoulder

shrine

siege

sieve

sign

Sikh

Sikhism

silhouette

simile

sincerely

situation

skein

sketch

skilful

software

soldier

soliloquy

solution

sorbet

source

sovereign

special

specification

spectrum

spirit

spiritual

spotlight

spreadsheet

squad

square

stage

stereotype

stomach

straight

strategy

strength

stupefy

suave

subordinate

subtraction

succeed

success

successful

suffix

sulphurous

supercilious

supersede

suppress

surely

surprise

surreptitious

survey

sycophant

symbol

symmetrical

symmetry

synagogue

synchronise

syncopation

synonym

synthesize

system

t

tabloid

tactic

technique

technology

temperature

temple

tempo

tension

tertiary

textile

texture

theatre

theatrical

theoretician

thermometer

thesaurus

threshold

tomorrow

tonne

tourism

tourist

tournament

trade

traitor

transport

transportation

triangle

triangular

triceps

truly

twelfth

tyranny

u

ubiquitous

ukulele

ululate

umbilical

umpire

unanimous

uncanny

unconscious

unctuous

undulate

unfortunately

unguent

unique

until

unwieldy

upholster

urban

usual

utmost

uxorious

v

vaccinate	veil	viable
vacillate	vengeance	vicious
vacuum	vertebrate	virus
vague	vertex	visage
variegated	vertical	vitamin
vaudeville	vertices	vocabulary
vegetable	vessel	vocal
vehement	vestige	volume
vehicle	veterinary	vowel

w

waive	Wednesday	wilful
wealth	weight	withhold
weather	weird	women
wedding	whinge	worship

x y z

xenophobia	yacht	zealous
xylophone	yearn	zephyr
	yeast	zeppelin
	yeoman	zucchini
	yield	zygote
	yogurt	

EXERCISE 1

SILENT LETTERS

Of the 26 letters in the alphabet only five are never silent!

f j q v x

b, c, n and **t** are sometimes silent.

Try to 'hear' the words in your head as you read them.

1 Underline the silent letters that are not pronounced but need to be written:

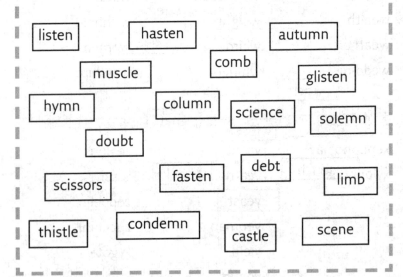

listen   hasten   autumn

muscle   comb   glisten

hymn   column   science   solemn

doubt

scissors   fasten   debt   limb

thistle   condemn   castle   scene

EXERCISE 1

h can be silent at the beginning of a word or with other letters. For example:

rhino   **Christmas**   **honest**   **hour**
white   **rhyme**

Some letters are silent with other letters.
- **w** is *always* silent before **r**
- **k** is *always* silent before **n**
- **g** is *always* silent before **n** at the beginning of a word and *sometimes* in the middle of a word

2 Sort these words into the table on the following page according to their silent letters.

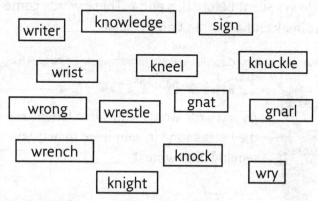

writer   knowledge   sign

wrist   kneel   knuckle

wrong   wrestle   gnat   gnarl

wrench   knock   wry

knight

EXERCISE 1

silent **w**	silent **k**	silent **g**

p is always silent before **n**, **s** and **t**. These words come from Greek and are often hard to spell!

Hints & Tips . . .

As you write words with silent letters, say the letter sound in your head to help you remember to write it.

EXERCISE 1

3 Look at these words, say them aloud and pronounce the silent letter.

pneumonia   **pterodactyl**
psalm   **psychology**

Cover each word, say it again sounding the silent letter and then write it. Did you spell it right?

FAQ ...

Why does English have so many silent letters?

Many words have been accepted into the English language from other languages, which is what makes English so complex.

Most of English's silent letters were originally pronounced either in English or in their own languages. For instance the first letter of 'knot' was clearly pronounced in Old English. Other words were adopted from Latin and gradually altered to fit the English language, with the spelling retaining some of its Latin features. 'Judge', for instance, has a silent 'd' that comes from the Latin *jūdicāre*, to pass judgement. Some of our silent letters come from French, most notably the initial silent letter 'h'. For example 'honest' comes from the Old French *honeste*.

EXERCISE 1

4 These 14 words are missing from the story opposite:

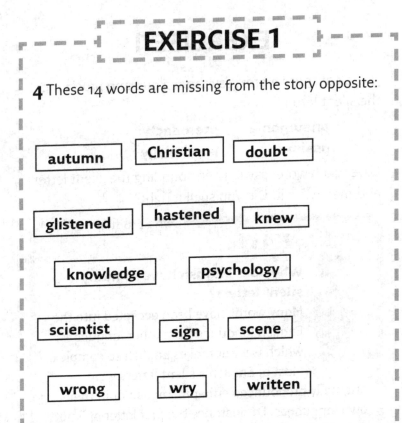

autumn	Christian	doubt
glistened	hastened	knew
knowledge	psychology	
scientist	sign	scene
wrong	wry	written

Look at the words, cover them up and try to write them in the story.

Voice each word, including the silent letter, in your head to help you spell it correctly.

Check how many you managed to spell correctly.

EXERCISE 1

_____ walked down the street. It was

an _____ day and the colourful trees

_____ in the morning light.

"What a wonderful _____," he said to himself.

He was a _____ who studied

_____ as a student. He was

looking for a road _____ to find

his tutor. He had _____ an essay

showing off his _____ and he was

keen to show his tutor. He _____ his

step. He mustn't take the _____ road.

He gave a _____ smile to himself; he

_____ he would get A+ for this work –

no _____ at all.

EXERCISE 1

HOMOPHONES

5 For each word, write another word that sounds the same but is spelled differently.

peace   *piece*

ceiling _____

board _____

break _____

vain _____

duel _____

led _____

flair _____

whole _____

steak _____

sent _____

right _____

altar _____

coarse _____

EXERCISE 1

6 For each pair of words in the paragraph, delete the one that is spelled incorrectly for the meaning.

John was busy preparing to open his music shop

in the High Street. He had already received his

license/licence from the record companies

who, in **principal/principle**, are happy for

small shops to sell their products. The biggest

hurdle to clear was to work out a **draught/**

draft agreement with the local **counsellor/**

councillor. It took time for him to **accept/**

except all **there/their** terms of trading, but

John took plenty of **advise/advice** and made

sure he got his **story/storey** straight. All the

EXERCISE 1

paperwork seemed to take **two/to/too** long,

but eventually the deal was signed. John had

always wanted to have his own shop because

he had a **flair/flare** for business. Next, he got

all the **stationery/stationary** and promotional

materials printed and he was ready to open his

doors. He was keeping his fingers crossed that

the opening day would see a **horde/hoard** of

people in a **cue/queue** outside.

CHAPTER TWO
The Spelling Rules You Really Need to Know

English has a small number of rules that underpin how certain words and types of words ought to be spelled. If you can learn these rules, you will be on your way to becoming a better and more confident speller. Don't be put off if the rule sounds complicated – look at the examples and you will begin to see spelling patterns emerging. Once you are familiar with these patterns, you can make a good attempt at guessing how a word ought to be spelled. Then you can check your dictionary to see if you've got it right.

Hints & Tips . . .

Make a habit of highlighting difficult vowel sounds.

Rule 1

- **-ize** or **-ise**?

The question of whether a verb should end in **-ize** or **-ise** is one that raises temperatures. Historically, both endings have always been used in English. The **-ize** spelling has been preferred in American English for over a century, and this had led some people to think that **-ize** is an Americanism, and object to its use in British English. Collins Dictionaries (and all other leading British dictionary publishers) show **-ize** as the main spelling form for these verbs, and **-ization** and **-izer** as the preferred forms of their derivatives. It is perfectly correct to use **-ise**, **-isation** and **-iser**. The most important thing is to be consistent and stick to one style.

ⓘ **The exceptions**

Some words are always spelled with **-ise**

advertise	devise	prise (meaning
advise	disguise	'to force open')
chastise	excise	revise
comprise	exercise	supervise
compromise	franchise	surprise
despise	improvise	televise

Some words are always spelled with **-ize**

capsize
prize (meaning 'to value highly')

Rule 2

- **i** before **e** except after **c**

When the letters **i** and **e** are combined to make the 'ee' sound, the **i** comes before the **e**.

Examples

achieve	field	relief
brief	hygiene	siege
chief	niece	thief

⚠ **The exceptions**

protein	seize

When they follow the letter **c** in a word, the **e** comes before the **i**.

Examples

ceiling	deceit	receipt
conceive	deceive	receive

Rule 3 - Suffixes

- Adding a suffix to words that end with a silent **e**

Many English words end with a silent **e** – that means the **e** is not pronounced. When you add a suffix that begins with a vowel onto these words, you drop the **e**.

Examples

abbreviate + -ion = abbreviation
appreciate + -ive = appreciative
desire + -able = desirable
guide + -ance = guidance
hope + -ing = hoping
response + -ible = responsible
ventilate + -ed = ventilated

① The exceptions

When the word ends in **ce** and sounds like **s** or the word ends in **ge** and sounds like **j**, you do not drop the final **e**.

notice + -able = noticeable
change + -able = changeable
outrage + -ous = outrageous

Rule 4 – Suffixes

- Adding a suffix to words that end with a consonant

In words of one syllable ending in a short vowel plus a consonant, you double the final consonant when you add a suffix that begins with a vowel.

Examples

run + ing = running
pot + ed = potted
thin + est = thinnest
swim + er = swimmer

In words of more than one syllable ending in a single vowel plus a consonant, if the stress is on the end of the word when it is pronounced, you double the final consonant when you add a suffix that begins with a vowel.

Examples

admit + -ance = admittance
begin + -ing = beginning
commit + -ed = committed
occur + -ence = occurrence

When you add a suffix that begins with a vowel to a word that ends in a single vowel plus **l** or **p**, you double the **l** or **p**.

Examples

appal + -ing = appalling
cancel + -ation = cancellation
dial + -er = dialler
fulfil + -ed = fulfilled
handicap + -ed = handicapped
kidnap + -er = kidnapper
slip + -age = slippage
wrap + -ing = wrapping

When you add a suffix that begins with **e**, **i** or **y** to a word that ends in **c**, you add a **k** after the **c**. This is to keep the hard **k** sound when it is pronounced.

Examples

mimic + -ed = mimicked
picnic + -ing = picnicking
panic + -y = panicky

(!) **The exceptions**

arc + -ed = arced
arc + -ing = arcing

Rule 5 - Suffixes

- Adding a suffix to words that end with **our**

When you add the suffixes **-ous** or **-ary** to a word that ends with **our**, you drop the **u** from **our**.

Examples

glamour + -ous = glamorous
humour + -ous = humorous
honour + -ary = honorary

Hints & Tips . . .

Learn spellings that are personal to you, your studies and your needs. At the back of each subject file or exercise book for school, stick a sheet of paper with a list of words you find difficult to spell.

Rule 6 – Suffixes

- Adding a suffix to words that end with **y**

When you add a suffix to a word that ends with a consonant plus **y**, you change the **y** to **i**.

Examples

apply + -ance = appliance
beauty + -ful = beautiful
crazy + -ly = crazily
happy + -ness = happiness
smelly + -er = smellier
woolly + -est = woolliest

⊘ **The exceptions**

In certain short adjectives that end with a consonant followed by **y**, you keep the **y** when you add the ending **-ly** to make an adverb.

shy + -ly = shyly
spry + -ly = spryly
wry + -ly = wryly

Rule 7 – Suffixes

- Adding the **-ly** suffix to words that end with **le**

When you make an adverb by adding the suffix **-ly** to an adjective that ends with **le**, you drop the **le** from the adjective.

Examples

gentle + -ly = gently
idle + -ly = idly
subtle + -ly = subtle

Hints & Tips . . .

There are only three verbs in English that end in -ceed:

succeed   proceed   exceed

All the other verbs with that sound end in -cede.

There's only one English verb that ends in -sede:

supersede

Rule 8 – Suffixes

- Words ending in **ful**

You always spell the suffix -**ful** with just one **l**.

Examples

beautiful	faithful	hopeful
cupful	grateful	painful

Hints & Tips . . .

The sound "full" at the end of a word is spelled with only one l.

For example:

careful   graceful   healthful   hopeful

The word "Full" itself is the only exception.

Rule 9 - Prefixes

- Words beginning with **al-**

When **all** and another word are joined to make an unhyphenated word, you drop the second **l**.

Examples

all + mighty = almighty
all + ready = already
all + though = although
all + together = altogether

If you are making a hyphenated form, you keep both **l**s.

Examples

all + important = all-important
all + inclusive = all-inclusive
all + powerful = all-powerful

Rule 10 – Plurals

- Making plurals of words that end with a consonant followed by **y**

When you make a plural of a word that ends with a consonant plus **y**, you change the **y** to **i** and add **-es**.

Examples

fairy + -es = fairies
pantry + -es = pantries
quality + -es = qualities
spy + -es = spies
story + -es = stories

Hints & Tips . . .

Writing a spelling down to see if it 'looks right' can help people with a strong visual memory.

Rule 11 - Plurals

- Making plurals of words that end with a vowel followed by **y**

When you make a plural of a word that ends with a vowel plus **y**, you add **-s**.

Examples

boy + -s = boys
day + -s = days
donkey + -s = donkeys
guy + -s = guys

Hints & Tips . . .

Break words down into small chunks to copy or spell. Start by taking 3-letter strings at a time and then build up your ability to remember more letters.

Rule 12 – Plurals

- Making plurals of words that end with **s**, **x**, **z**, **sh** or **ch**

When you make a plural of a word that ends with **s**, **x**, **z**, **sh** or **ch**, you add **-es**.

Examples

bus + -es = buses
kiss + -es = kisses
lens + -es = lenses
fox + -es = foxes
jinx + -es = jinxes
buzz + es = buzzes
rash + -es = rashes
match + -es = matches
ranch + -es = ranches

Rule 13 - Plurals

• Making plurals of words that end with **eau**

When you make a plural of a word that ends with **eau**, you add **-x** or **-s**. Words that end with **eau** are French words that have come into English. The **-x** ending is the French plural, and the **-s** ending is the English one. Both forms are acceptable for these words.

Examples

bureau + -x = bureaux
bureaus + -s = bureaus
chateau + -x = chateaux
chateau + -s = chateaus
gateau + -x = gateaux
gateau + -s = gateaus

Hints & Tips . . .

Different people learn spelling in different ways. Find out how you learn best.

Rule 14 – Plurals

- Making plurals of words that end with a single **o**

When you make a plural of a word that ends with a single **o**, you add **-s**.

Examples

memo + -s = memos
solo + -s = solos
taco + -s = tacos
zero + -s = zeros

(!) The exceptions

There are a number of words that end with a single **o** that add **-es** when they are plural.

echo + -es = echoes
hero + -es = heroes
potato + -es = potatoes
tomato + -es = tomatoes
veto + -es = vetoes

EXERCISE 2

VOWEL CHOICES

i before e and all that – the vowel choices for long vowel sounds can be confusing!

	opening syllable	inside a word	ending
Long a	a *agent*	a-e ai eigh ei *lake brain sleigh vein*	ay ey *day they*
Long e	e *equal*	ee ea ie e-e ei *need peach field these ceiling*	ee ey *tree key*
Long i	i *idea*	i-e igh y y-e *nine light cycle tyre*	y lie *sky lie*
Long o	o *only*	o-e oa *home cloak*	ow oe *glow toe*
Long u	u *union*	u-e eu *cube feud*	ew ue *crew argue*

EXERCISE 2

1   Fill in the missing ā sounds

e.g. When we got to the l_k_, it started to r__n.

The young prince's r_____gn as King began when
he bec_m_ _____ teen. He promised to honour
and ob _____ and to conv _____ the right w_____
for the country to beh_v_.

2   Fill in the missing e sounds

The l_____der of the local council agr_____d that
the commit_____ should have a good r_____son to
delay its next m_____ting. It should not dec_____ve
the public or imp_d_ the work of the attorn_____
who was costing a lot of mon_____ .

EXERCISE 2

3 Fill in the missing **i** sounds

The p_thon was so powerful it paral_sed its prey.
The zoo keeper had to _dentif_ the wildl_f_ that
d____d and f_l_ a report. None of the animals
could be rev_v_d.

4 Fill in the missing **o** sounds

The g____t was al_n_ in the mead____ . It
ch_k_d on a piece of t____st it had ch_s_n to
swall____ .

5 Fill in the missing **u** sounds

The stat____ was _s_less and had no val____.
It was moved to a n____ ven____ to subd____
those who took the vi____ that the _nited
Nations didn't have a cl____ about art.

EXERCISE 2

PLURALS

Singular means one. **Plural** means more than one.
Do not add an apostrophe when making a plural!

Spelling	Rule	Example
Most nouns	Add **s**	cat → cat**s**
Nouns ending in a vowel and **y**	Add **s**	boy → boy**s**
Nouns ending in a consonant and **y**	Change **y** to **ie** and add **s**	party → part**ies**
Nouns ending in **s**, **x**, **z**, **sh** or **ch**	Add **es**	boss → boss**es** fox → fox**es** mush → mush**es** church → church**es**
Most nouns ending in **f** and some ending in **fe**	Change **f** to **ves**	leaf → lea**ves** life → li**ves**
Nouns ending in a vowel plus **o**, **eo**, **io**, **oo**	Add **s**	rodeo → rodeo**s** studio → studio**s** cuckoo → cuckoo**s**
Nouns ending in **o** Learn the exceptions	Add **s** or **es**	piano → piano**s** tomato → tomato**es**
Nouns ending in **eau** (from French)	Add **x** (French) or **s** (English)	chateau → chateau**x** chateau → chateau**s**

EXERCISE 2

(!)   There are some exceptions! Check by reading the section called 'The spelling rules you really need to know' on pages 47–62 to check you know them!

6 Make plurals of these words.

Singular	Plural
horse	→
gateau	→
curry	→
knife	→
family	→
video	→
match	→

EXERCISE 2

7 Rewrite this paragraph changing the singular nouns into plurals.

Remember other words such as verbs and pronouns will have to change too!

The old lady looked at her photo. It showed her family when they were young.
It brought back a happy memory. She had enjoyed her party and seemed not to have one worry. How her life had changed.
The story she would tell her grandchildren!

The old _____ looked at _____ _____. _____

showed _____ _____ when they were young.

_____ brought back _____ happy _____. _____

had enjoyed _____ _____ and seemed not to have

___ _____. How _____ _____ had changed. The

_____ _____ would tell _____ grandchildren!

EXERCISE 2

8 Some nouns have irregular plurals.

Do you know the plurals of these nouns?

mouse	fungus	die
sheep	ox	louse

9 There are 20 spelling mistakes of plurals in the paragraph below. Can you spot them?

The tired farmer looked out of the window across the rooves of the outbuildings and to the vallies of his farm. The muted echos of noisy cowes could be heard. The leafs were changing from green to red, silhouetted against the evening skys. It was harvest time. He should have been digging potatos and tending his tomatos in the greenhouse's, but the farmer had bigger worrys: protecting his chicken's from the wolfs who were hiding in the bushs surrounding the field's. The farmer and his friend has spent the night in their lorrys hoping to scare the wolfs away. They kept themselfs awake by eating loafs of bread. But the animal's were too clever. More chicken's died that night and the crisis carried on.

CHAPTER THREE
Ways to Improve Your Spelling

When you are practising your spelling, there are various strategies you can use to help.

1. A good way to learn spellings is to use the 'Look, Say, Cover, Write, Check' method.

Look at the word carefully.
Say the word aloud to yourself, listening to how it sounds.
Cover the word and try to remember what it looks like.
Write the word.
Check what you have written to see if you got it right.

2. Break the word up into its syllables, and sound them out, pronouncing even the silent letters. For example:

dictionary = dic + tion + ar + y
handkerchief = hand +ker + chief
Wednesday = Wed + nes +day
ecstasy = ec + sta + sy

remember = re + mem + ber
laboratory = lab + or + a + tor + y
raspberry = rasp + berry
business = bus + i + ness

Get into the habit of looking at words in this way and you will find it easier to remember how to spell them.

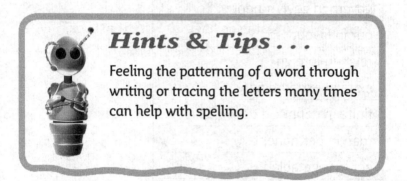

Hints & Tips . . .

Feeling the patterning of a word through writing or tracing the letters many times can help with spelling.

3. Look for patterns and relations between words. If there is word you do not know how to spell, try to think of another word that is perhaps related to it. For example:

muscle + muscular
excel + excellent
occur + occurrence
irritable + irritate

minuscule + minute
succeed + successful
rhyme + rhythm
precede + precedent

4. Look for words within words. For example:

govern in government
our in favour
reign in foreign
extra in extraordinary
finite in definite
man in permanent
get in vegetable
leg in phlegm
vile in privilege

5. Make use of mnemonics. A mnemonic is a way of remembering something. The word comes from Greek *mnēmonikos*, which itself comes from *mnēmōn* meaning 'mindful'. A mnemonic can be a rhyme or sentence that helps you remember anything, not just spelling. You may already know mnemonics for other things, for example:

- **R**ichard **of Y**ork **g**ave **b**attle **in v**ain
  = red orange yellow green blue indigo violet (the colours of the rainbow in order)

- **A**ngry **e**lephants **in o**range **u**nderwear
  = **A E I O U** (the vowels of the English alphabet)

There are different kinds of mnemonics.

(a) Initial letter mnemonics
In this, the word is spelt out by the initial letters of the words in a sentence or phrase. For example:

- **B**ig **e**lephants **a**re **u**seful **t**o **I**ndians **f**or **u**nloading **l**ogs
  = beautiful

- **B**ig **e**ars **a**re **u**seful **t**o you
  = beauty

- **B**ig **e**lephants **c**an **a**lways **u**nderstand **s**mall **e**lephants
  = because

- **B**ig **u**nsinkable **o**cean **y**acht
  = buoy

- **C**itizens **h**ave **a**bolished **o**ur **s**ystem
  = chaos

- **E**dith **i**s **g**oing **h**ome **t**o **H**enry
  = eighth

- **G**reat **A**unt **U**na **g**rows **e**ggplants
  = gauge

- **G**et **r**ich **a**nd **p**lay **h**ard
  = graph

- **H**appy **E**dward **is** **r**ich
  = heir

- **I** **n**ever **d**abble **i**n **c**riminal **t**hings
  = indict

- **L**ouise **is** **a**lways **in** **s**ome **o**ld **n**ightdress
  = liaison

- **M**y **n**ephew **E**ric **m**emorizes **o**dd **n**umbers **in** **c**lass
  = mnemonic

- **R**oger **h**ates **y**our **t**errible **h**eavy **m**etal
  = rhythm

- **U**gly **s**wan **u**ses **a** **l**ipstick
  = usual

Try making up your own initial letter mnemonics using the names of your friends, pets or favourite sports stars:

- **C**hris **H**oy **r**iding **in** **s**peed **t**rial **m**oves **a**way **s**wiftly
  = Christmas

(b) Partial initial letter mnemonics

These are reminders of the tricky bits of certain words. For example:

- accelerate
  = if it can **acceler**ate, **a** **c**ar **c**an **e**asily **l**ead **e**very **r**ace

- accommodation
  = the a**cc**o**mm**odation has two **c**ots and two
  mattresses

- attach
  = att**ach a c**oat **h**ook to the wall

- broccoli
  = bro**cc**oli **c**ures **c**oli**c**

- dachshund
  = **da**chshunds **ch**ase **sh**eep through the **und**ergrowth

- familiar
  = someone who is famil**iar** **is** **a** **r**egular

- jodhpurs
  = you wear jo**dh**purs when you ride a **d**appled **h**orse

- necessary
  = it is ne**cess**ary to wear one **c**ardigan but two **s**ocks

- neurotic
  = the government is n**eu**rotic about the **E**uropean
  Union

- paraffin
  = para**ff**in **r**eally **f**uels **f**ires

- possess
  = you must po**ssess** two **s**ocks and two **s**hoes

- surgeon
  = sur**geo**ns graft **e**ars **on**

- vain
  = **va**in is **v**ery **a**rrogant

- vein
  = **ve**in is a **ve**ssel

(c) Partial mnemonics

These remind us of words or syllables that are contained within the problem word. For example:

- abattoir
  = there may be **a battl**e in an **abatt**oir

- address
  = **add** your **add**ress

- Arctic
  = there an **arc** in the **Arc**tic

- attendance
  = you **dance** atten**dance** on someone

- bachelor
  = was **Bach** a **bach**elor?

- beggar
  = there is a beg**gar** in the **gar**den

- business
  = it's none of your **busi**ness what **bus I** get

- cemetery
  = a cemet**ery** is v**ery** scary

- colonel
  = the co**lonel** is **lonel**y

- comparison
  = there's no com**paris**on with **Paris**

- conscience
  = you don't have a **conscience** if you **con science**

- demeanour
  = de**meanour** can **mean our** behaviour

- derogatory
  = he made derog**atory** remarks about **a Tory**

- dilemma
  = **Emma** is in a dil**emma**

- elegant
  = what an e**legant leg Ant**onia has

- environment
  = there is **iron** in the envi**ron**ment

- etiquette
  = the **que**en is an expert on eti**que**tte

- fowl
  = an **owl** is a f**owl**

- friend
  = my **frie**nd likes **frie**s

- hearse
  = I didn't **hear** the **hear**se

- hideous
  = **hide** those **hide**ous things

- hospital
  = **Al** is in hospit**al**

- Hungary
  = **Gary** is from Hun**gary**

- hungry
  = I get an**gry** when I'm hun**gry**

- intelligent
  = I can **tell** the **gent** is in**tell**i**g**ent

- interrupt
  = it is **terri**bly rude to in**terr**upt

- laundry
  = wash and **dry** your clothes at the laun**dry**

- massacre
  = a **mass** of crops in every **acre**

- mathematics
  = teach **them** ma**them**atics

- niece
  = my **nie**ce is **ni**ce

- optimistic
  = **Tim** is op**tim**istic

- originally
  = I ori**gin**ally asked for **gin**

- parliament
  = **Liam** is in par**liam**ent

- principal
  = **pal** up with the princi**pal** and the princi**pal** staff

- principle
  = first you must **le**arn the princip**le**s

- rehearsal
  = I **hear** there is a re**hear**sal

- satellite
  = **tell** me about the sa**tell**ite

- secretary
  = a **secret**ary must be able to keep a **secret**

- shepherd
  = the job of a shep**herd** is to **herd** sheep

- tragedy
  = I **raged** at the **traged**y of it

- viscount
  = a v**iscount is count**ed an aristocrat

(d) Other mnemonics

Some mnemonics can help with the spellings of several words at once:

Eddy **A**nt thinks m**ea**t is a gr**ea**t tr**ea**t to **ea**t (-ea-)

Elaine and **E**mily shout **ee** when they m**ee**t to gr**ee**t each other (-ee-)

King **Ia**n went to parl**ia**ment in a carr**ia**ge for his marr**ia**ge (-ia-)

Hints & Tips . . .

Accommodation and accommodate have two *c*s, but remember they have two *m*s as well.

EXERCISE 3

Look for ways to make spelling easier for you.

SYLLABLES

• Break words down into manageable chunks or syllables.

• Say the chunks aloud with exaggerated pronunciation.

• Let your ears and mouth help your eyes learn spellings.

• Remember every syllable needs a vowel or a vowel sound!

• Check that the number of chunks or syllables corresponds with what you write down.

e.g. rem/em/ber = 3 syllables ✔ not rem/ber ✘

diff/er/ence =3 syllables
in/ter/es/ting = 4 syllables

EXERCISE 3

1 These words are all two syllable words. Can you join up the starts and ends of all the words to make words you might hear at school?

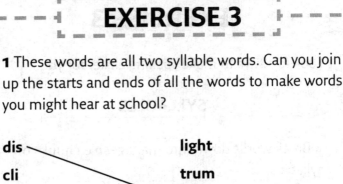

dis	light
cli	trum
in	play
spec	sion
ten	fix
ex	fix
pre	las
at	mate
con	scape
high	flict
land	ware
hard	word
pass	lect
ref	sorb
suf	change
ab	sect

EXERCISE 3

In which subjects might you use these words?

ART: _____
_____

D&T: _____
_____

ENGLISH: _____
_____

GEOG: _____
_____

HIST: _____
_____

IT: _____
_____

MATHS: _____
_____

SCIENCE: _____
_____

EXERCISE 3

2 Unscramble these subject words.

Look, say (aloud pronouncing the syllables), cover, and rewrite them in their correct columns opposite. Now check. Did you get them right?

- tor/a/pred • es/tant/Prot • pec/pers/tive
- tron/el/ec/ic • ture/temp/a/er
- tip/mul/ca/li/tion • fer/cir/ence/cum
- tion/spec/a/if/ic • phor/a/met
- tat/hab/i • tory/a/or/lab • tor/den/om/a/in
- a/prop/a/gand • ac/in/ter/tive
- al/quad/at/er/ril • sion/dim/en
- nent/com/po/ • ant/son/con
- a/all/it/tion/er • tude/i/long
- ment/gov/ern • tive/a/neg
- at/il/equ/al/er • tus/app/a/ar
- if/per/son/a/tion/ic • in/ture/fra/struc
- ia/ment/parl • tion/pres/ta/en
- al/in/nat/ion/ter • u/cab/vo/lar/y
- ma/ex/tion/cla

EXERCISE 3

Art	
D&T	
English	
Geography	
History	
IT	
Maths	
Science	

EXERCISE 3

PATTERNS AND RELATIONS WITHIN WORDS

Look for root words within words.

e.g. **act** → **act**ion – **act**ivity – re**act** – re**act**ion

irritate → irritable

profession → professionally

contaminate → contamination

3 How many words can you make from these root words?

child _____

_____

_____

_____

take _____

_____

_____

public _____

_____

_____

EXERCISE 3

bore _____

_____

_____

pass _____

_____

_____

sign _____

_____

_____

cover _____

_____

_____

medic _____

_____

_____

electric _____

_____

_____

give _____

_____

_____

EXERCISE 3

Add and take away prefixes and suffixes and build on the smaller root words.

e.g. un/help/ful, dis/appoint/ment

Adding suffixes like this will help you to remember unsaid letters.

e.g. jump/ed, happen/ed

LITTLE WORDS WITHIN BIG WORDS

Look for little words within big words.

sOLDier   exPLANation favOURite
conSCIENCE
KNOWledge misCHIEF   outRAGEous

Do you know any other little words that are within big words?

Write them in a sentence.

EXERCISE 3

MNEMONICS

See the beginning of this chapter, pages 73–80, for common mnemonics.

Make a list of the words you frequently misspell. Then make up mnemonics of your own to try to remember how to spell them.

CHAPTER FOUR
Where Does English Spelling Come From?

Dozens of languages have contributed words to English.

Old English

Old English, or Anglo-Saxon as it is also known, was spoken in parts of England and Scotland between the 5th and 12th centuries. It developed into Middle English, then Early Modern English and then into the Modern English we speak today.

English words from Anglo-Saxon tend to be short (either one or two syllables). They relate to areas such as the human body, animals, farming, the weather, family relationships, colours, landscape features, and human activities such as cooking, eating, sewing, hunting and carpentry.

Some examples are:

a

abide
about
above
acorn
acre
after
again
ago
ale
alive
all
and
apple
arm
ask
awake
axe

b

back
bare
barley
barn
bath
beat
bed
bear
beard
begin
believe
belly
beneath
berry
bind
bird
bite
blaze
black
blind
blood
body
bone
bottom
bowl
brain
bring
brother
brown
burn

c

can
care
carve
check
chicken
child
choose
claw
clean
climb
cloud
cold
comb
come
corn
cough
cow
cradle
craft
crow
cunning
cup

d

daft
dairy
daisy
dark
daughter
day
dead

deaf
death
deep
deer
die
dish
do
dog
door
drink
drop
drunk
dry
duck
dusk

e

each
ear
earth
east
eat
edge
elbow
empty
end
enough
evening

evil
eye

f

fair
fall
fast
father
fear
feather
fern
fetch
few
field
fight
find
finger
fish
fleece
flood
fly
folk
food
foot
for
fox
free
friend

frog
frost

g

game
gate
gather
gift
give
glad
go
god
gold
good
goose
grass
green
ground
grow

h

hail
hair
hammer
hand
harbour
hard

harvest
hate
hay
head
heart
heaven
hedge
hell
help
hen
herring
high
hill
hit
hollow
holy
honey
horn
horse
hot
house
hunger
hunt
husband

i

I
ice

if
in
island
it
itch

k

keen
keep
kind
king
kiss
knee
knife
knot
know

l

ladder
ladle
lamb
land
last
laugh
leaf
leap
leek

less
life
light
lip
listen
long
lord
lot
loud
love

m

make
man
many
mare
mark
marsh
me
meadow
meal
meat
might
milk
mist
moon
mother
mouse

mouth
much

n

nail
name
narrow
near
neck
need
needle
neigh
nest
net
never
night
no
north
nostril
now
nut

o

oak
of
old
on

open
orchard
oven
over
owl
ox

p

paddock
pail
path
pin
pipe
plant
play
plough
poppy
pretty
priest

q

queen
quick

r

rag
rain

ram
rat
read
reap
red
ride
right
ripe
rock
roof
root
run

s

sad
salt
sand
say
scrape
scythe
sea
see
seek
send
sew
shadow
sharp
sheep

shirt
shoe
shut
sick
side
sin
sing
sister
sit
skin
sleep
snail
son
sore
soul
south
spade
speak
speed
spin
spoon
stag
star
steal
steep
stone
storm
straw

stream
strong
sun
sweat
swim
sword

t

tail
take
teach
tell
thank
the
thick
thief
thigh
thimble
thing
thirst
thorn
thread
throat
throw
thumb
tie
time
toad

today
tomorrow
tongue
tool
tooth
trap
tree
true
turn
twig

u

udder
under
up
us

v

vat

w

wag
wake
walk
wall
walnut
warm

wart

wash

water

way

weapon

weather

weave

weed

well

west

white

winter

wise

witch

with

wolf

woman

wood

word

world

wrestle

wring

wrist

write

wrong

y

yard

yarn

yawn

year

yellow

yes

yew

yolk

you

young

Hints & Tips . . .

Break up words and exaggerate their pronunciation in your head, for example, bus-i-ness or Wed-nes-day

Old Norse

In the 9th and 10th centuries, the British Isles were subjected to repeated invasions by Vikings (or Norsemen) from Scandinavia. The invaders spoke Old Norse, a Germanic language that was related to Old English. Many of these invaders settled in Britain and introduced their own words that were later absorbed into English.

Some examples are:

a

aloft
anger
ankle
awe
awkward

b

bag
ball
bark
beaker
birth
bulk

c

cake
cart

club
creek

d

daze
dirt
down
dregs
drift
droop

e

eddy
egg

f

filly
flat

fling
fluster
force
freckle

g

gallows
gap
gape
gasp
gelding
glitter
gosling
gust

h

happy
hoarse

i

ill

k

keel
kettle
kindle

l

lad
leak
leg
lift
loan
loose
low

m

meek
mire
mistake
murk

o

odd

r

race
raise
reindeer
rid
rotten
rune

s

sag
saga
same
scalp
scar
scare
scold
scrap
seem
skill
skirt
sky
sly
stern

t

tang
tern

tether
their
they
thrive
tight
trust

u

ugly

v

vole

w

wail
want
whirl
whisker
window
wreck

y

yowl

Latin

Latin has had a greater influence over the vocabulary of English than any other language. Latin words have come into English at various stages throughout history: during the time of the first Christian missionaries in the 6th and 7th centuries; after the Norman Conquest of 1066; during the English Renaissance (around 1500–1650); and then during the 17th and 18th centuries with the growth in scientific knowledge. Even today, newly discovered animals are given Latin names.

Here is a very small sample of Latin words in everyday English:

a

abbey
abbreviate
ability
abolish
absent
absolute
accent
accident
accuse
acid
act
add
address
admit
adore
adventure
affect
age
alien
allow
ambition
amiable
animal
appeal
aquatic
arch
area
army
art
assert
audible

b

balance
base
battle
beast
beauty
bisect
blame
boil
bonus
bottle
branch
burglar

c

cabin
cage
calendar
calm
campaign
cancer
cap
captain
carnivore
carpet
carry
castle
cease
cellar
century
chance
charm
cheese
circle
city
class
coast
coffin
colour
commence
companion
conceal
condition
confiscate
conifer
consult
contribute
copy
correspond
credit
cross
cucumber
cure

d

damage
data
decimal
decorate
delicious
dense
describe
design
diamond
diary
digit
direct
dissolve
diva
divorce
doctor
double
duet

e

eagle
edible
educate
efficient
ego
elegant
emotion
empire
enemy
erase
error
estimate
event
example
excuse
exhaust
expert
extract

f

fabric
face

fail
false
fame
family
fascinate
favour
feast
female
fiction
fierce
figure
finish
flower
focus
forest
fork
fragile
fraud
front
fume
fury

g

gem
gender
genius
germ
glacier

glue
gradual
gravity
gutter

h

habit
habitat
hallucinate
heir
herb
hibernate
homicide
honest
horrible
hospital
hour

i

identity
ignite
ignore
illusion
image
immediate
impertinent
important

include
increase
industry
infant
ingredient
injury
insect
instrument
intelligence
interval
invent
irritate

j

janitor
jealous
jelly
joke
joy
judge
justice

k

kennel
kiln
kitchen

l

laboratory
labour
lace
lake
language
large
lavatory
legal
legend
letter
liberal
library
local
lunatic
luxury

m

machine
major
mammal
manicure
map
marine
maternal
mention
merit
mineral
minor
misery
mix
modest
money
mortal
mule
mute

m

narrate
nation
navigate
necessary
nominate
normal
noun
nude
number

o

obese
object
obscene
occasion
offend
oil
omen
onion
oppose
order
ovary

p

page
pain
paper
parent
paternal
pattern
peach
pedicure
pencil
penicillin
people
person
persuade
picture
plague
poison
pollute
poor
pork
posse

pray
predict
pregnant
prevent
primary
private
profession
promise
prove
province
public
puncture
pupil
pus

reason
receive
redundant
reflect
relax
remote
reptile
respect
result
rival
rose
rota
ruby
rude
rural

secret
senile
sense
serial
serpent
sex
sign
situate
slave
solid
sound
space
spirit
statue
sterile
story
student
stupid
subdue
subscribe
suburb
sudden
suicide
superb
superstition
support
syllabus

q

qualify
quality
quantity
query
quiet

r

rabies
radio
radish
rapid

s

saint
salary
salmon
sanction
satire
savage
scalpel
schedule
science
script
sculpture

t

table
tact
tarantula
tax
telescope
temperature
tempt
tepid
text
tile
timid
tinsel
tonsil
torture
tractor
tradition
transfer
triangle
tribute
tube

u

ulcer
ultimate
uncle
uniform
union
urban
urge
use

v

vacant
vaccine
valiant
valley
value
variety
vehicle
ventilate
venue
verb
versatile
veteran
viaduct
vicar
victim
violence
virus
visual
vomit
vote
voyage

w

waste
wine

Hints & Tips . . .

Make a habit of looking up any words you are doubtful about in a reliable dictionary, such as *Collins School Dictionary*

Greek

Most of the Greek words in the English language come from Ancient Greek. These are either whole words, new words created by combining Greek words together, or Greek prefixes and suffixes that we have added to other words. An example of this is **television**, which comes from the Greek *tele* meaning 'from afar' and the Latin *visio* meaning 'see'.

Some come from Medieval Greek, such as **diaper**, **talisman** and **tartar**, and Modern Greek continues to supply words to English. These mainly relate to Greek foods and drinks that have spread outside Greece, for example **feta**, **filo**, **moussaka**, **ouzo**, **retsina** and **taramasalata**.

Here are a few Greek words that have entered the English lexicon (which comes from the Greek *lexis* meaning 'word'):

a

abyss
academy
acrobat
aerial
agony
air
almond
alphabet

anchor
angel
arithmetic
athlete
atom
autograph

b

bacteria

basis
bible
bishop
bomb
bulb

c

camel
cardiac

carrot
catapult
category
cemetery
centre
chorus
church
climate
comic
crocodile
cube
cycle

d

decade
democracy
devil
diagnosis
diagram
dinosaur
dolphin
dynamite

e

ebony
eccentric
ecology

economy
elastic
embryo
emphasis
energy
epidemic
episode
ethic
ethnic
exotic

f

fantasy
feta
filo

g

gangrene
gas
genesis
giant
gorilla
grammar
gymnasium

h

haemorrhage

harmony
helicopter
hermit
hero
hierarchy
history
holocaust
hormone
hygiene
hysteria

i

icon
idea
idiot
irony
isobar

j

jot

k

kaleidoscope
kerosene
kinetic
lamp

l

larynx
leper
lexicon
liquorice
logarithm
lyric

m

magic
magnet
marble
mechanic
melody
metal
meteor
method
mime
mint
monarch
monologue
moussaka
music
mystery

n

narcotic

nausea
nautical
nectar
neuron
nomad

o

oasis
octopus
opal
optic
orchestra
orphan
ouzo
ozone

p

paediatrics
pancreas
panic
pantomime
paradise
paralysis
patriot
petal
pharmacy
phase

philosophy
phobia
pirate
planet
plastic
pneumonia
poem
practice
problem
protein
psyche
pylon

q

quince

r

retsina
rhapsody
rhetoric
rhinoceros
rhythm

s

sandal
sarcasm
scandal

scene
scheme
school
skeleton
sock
sphere
stadium
stomach
strangle
surgery
symbol
system

t

talisman
taramasalata
technique
technology
telephone
theatre
theme
theory
throne
tiger
tomb
toxic

treasure
type

x

xenophobia

z

zeal
zodiac

French

The main period for the introduction of French words into English was after the Norman Conquest of 1066. For the next 300 or so years, the language of the royal court, and therefore of authority, was Norman, a variety of French. The ruling classes spoke what came to be known as Anglo-Norman, while the rest of the population (the peasants!) carried on speaking English. French became the language of law and government. This carried on until about the end of the 14th century when English reasserted itself as the language of authority. But French had made its mark on English and many of its words remain in use in English today. Some modern French

words have also been absorbed into English.
Some examples of French words in English are:

a

abandon
account
achieve
adjourn
allegiance
alliance
aperitif
apron
arrange
assemble
attorney
avalanche

b

bacon
bail
bandage
basin
beef
beret
blouse
bouquet
brilliant

c

café
cattle
chalet
coat
console
control
couch
courgette
courtesy
cricket
croissant
cry

d

dab
dainty
dance
defeat
depart
disease
dress
drug

e

easy
éclair
employ
enjoy
envelope
essay

f

faint
fairy
farm
fee
finance
flavour
frown
furniture

g

gain
gallery
garage
garden
genre

goblin
grape
grocer
guard

h

hatch
haunt
helmet
hotel
hurt

i

inherit
ink
interfere
issue

j

jacket
jail
jewel
jolly
journey
juggle
juice
jury

k

kerb
kitten

l

label
larder
lesson
lieutenant
live
locket

m

mackerel
mail
mallet
manner
manure
march
medal
menu
message
mitten
moist
mutiny

n

nice
nuisance
nutmeg

o

oboe
omelette

p

packet
panel
parachute
parliament
party
passage
peasant
petty
picnic
platform
pleasant
poultry
print
proud
puppy

q

quaint
quay
quiche
quit

r

rail
raisin
random
razor
recruit
reign
remove
rescue
restaurant
riot
river
romance
royal

s

salad
saucer
sausage
scarce
scissors
search
shock
size
soldier
sound
soup
spice
stuff
surprise

t

tailor
tambourine
tarot
taste
tissue
toilet
torch
towel
treaty
trick
trouble

tunnel

u

umpire

v

valet
varnish
velvet
vinegar
vogue
wafer
wage
warrior
zest

German

English and German are both derived from the same language family so there are many words in English that can be described as 'Germanic' in origin. However, words from Modern German have also been absorbed into English within the last century or so.

For example:

a

abseil
accordion
angst

b

bismuth
blitzkrieg
bum

c

caffeine
cartel
chorale

d

dachshund
delicatessen

doppelgänger
drill

e

edelweiss
ersatz

f

feldspar
fest
flak
frankfurter

g

gene
glockenspiel
graphite

h

halt
hamburger
hamster

k

kaput
kindergarten
kitsch

l

lager
leitmotif
lied

m

meerschaum
melamine

n

nickel
noodle

p

poltergeist
pretzel
pumpernickel
putsch

q

quartz

r

riesling

rottweiler
rucksack

s

sabre
Schadenfreude
schnapps
schnauzer
snorkel
spanner
spiel
strafe
stroll
strudel
swindle

u

umlaut

w

waltz

y

Yiddish
yodel

z

Zeitgeist
zigzag
zinc

Italian

Italian has provided English with words relating to a variety of areas, but it has been particularly productive in the fields of music, food, art and architecture, reflecting the influence that Italians have had in these areas. Some examples of Italian words in English are:

a

adagio
alert
allegro
alto
altruism
antic
antipasto
aria
arpeggio
attack

b

balcony
ballet
bandit
bassoon
bimbo
bizarre
broccoli

bruschetta
bulletin

c

cadenza
cameo
cannelloni
cannon
cappuccino
carnival
cartoon
cash
cavalry
chipolata
concerto
confetti
crescendo

d

ditto

e

embarrass
espresso
extravaganza

f

falsetto
fiasco
finale
forte
fresco

g

gesso
ghetto
gondola
graffiti
grotto

i

influenza

l

largo
lasagne
lento
libretto
loggia

m

macaroni
mandolin
manifesto
marzipan
mascarpone
mezzanine
minestrone
motto
mozzarella

n

novella

o

oratorio

p

panache
paparazzo
parmesan
pasta
patina
pergola
piano
pizza
portfolio
propaganda

q

quartet
quintet

r

ravioli
regatta
replica
ricotta
risotto
rotunda

s

salami

scampi
scenario
scherzo
semolina
sonata
soprano
spaghetti
stanza
stiletto
studio

t

tagliatelle
tempo
terracotta
timpani
tombola
trampoline
trio
trombone

u

umbrella

v

vendetta
vermicelli

violin
vista
volcano

z

zabaglione
zany

zucchini

Spanish

Spanish words have come into English from Spain and the Spanish-speaking countries of South and Central America.

Some examples are:

a

abalone
alligator
anchovy
armadillo
avocado

b

balsa
barracuda
bodega
bolero
bonanza
breeze
bronco
busker

c

cafeteria
cannibal
canyon
cargo
cask
castanets
cedilla
cigar
cockroach
conga
corral

d

desperado
doubloon

e

embargo

f

fajitas
fiesta
flamenco
flotilla

g

galleon
garrotte
grenade
guerrilla
guitar

h

hammock
hurricane

i

indigo

j

jojoba
junta

m

machete
machismo
maize
mambo
marijuana
mascara
matador
mosquito

p

palomino
papaya

parakeet
patio
pimento
poncho
pronto

q

quinine

r

renegade
rodeo
rumba

s

salsa
sangria
sherry
sierra
silo
sombrero
stampede
stockade

t

taco
tango
tapas
tilde
tobacco
toreador
tornado
tortilla
tuna

v

vamoose
vanilla
vigilante

z

zebra

Dutch

Another language that is closely related to English and German, Dutch has contributed an interesting variety of words to English vocabulary over the years.

For example:

a

advocaat
Afrikaans

b

block
bluff
boss
brandy
brawl

c

coleslaw
commando
cookie
cruise

d

dabble
decoy

domineering
dope
dunderhead

e

easel
eland
etch

f

filibuster
freebooter
frolic

g

gherkin
gin

h

harpoon

hustle

k

kink

m

mangle
meerkat

n

nasty

p

pinkie
plunder
poppycock

r

rant
roster

s

sleigh
slim
sloop
snoop
snuff

spook
stoop
swirl

t

tattoo
trigger

w

waffle
wagon
walrus

Arabic

Many of the Arabic words that have become part of the English language relate to mathematics, science and philosophy, showing Arabic to be a language of culture and learning. It is also the religious language of Islam. A few of the Arabic words firmly established in English are:

a

alchemy
alcohol
alfalfa
algebra
alkali
Arab
artichoke
assassin
azure

b

Bedouin
burqa

c

calibre
candy
carafe
casbah
cipher
couscous
crimson

e

elixir
emir

f

fakir

g

gazelle
genie
ghoul
giraffe

h

hajj
halal
halloumi

harem
hazard
henna

i

imam
intifada
Islam

j

jellaba

k

kebab
kohl
Koran

l

lemon
lime
loofah

m

magazine
mattress
minaret
monsoon
mosque
muezzin
mullah
Muslim

n

nadir

o

orange

p

popinjay

s

saffron

senna
sheikh
sofa
souk
spinach
sultan
syrup

t

tahini
tamarind
tariff

y

yashmak

z

zenith
zero

Asian languages

The English language came into contact with the languages of the Asian subcontinent when trade began between Britain and India. Many words were borrowed from these languages during the time of the British Raj. Even today, culinary and other cultural terms from India and Pakistan come into English regularly.

Borrowed words include:

Sanskrit

a

Aryan
ashram
avatar

b

Brahman

d

dharma

g

Gurkha

k

karma

m

mahatma
mandarin
mantra

n

nirvana

s

sandalwood
swastika

y

yoga

Hindi

a

ayah

b

bandanna
bangle
basmati
bhaji
bhangra
Blighty
bungalow

c

chapatti
cheetah
chintz
chit
chukka
chutney
cot
cummerbund
cushy

d

desi
dhal

g

ghee
guru
gymkhana

h

howdah

j

juggernaut
jungle

k

kedgeree
kukri

l

loot

m

maharaja
maharani
maharishi
mahout
mynah

n

nabob
nan
nawab

p

poppadom
pukka
pundit
punkah
purdah
puttee

r

raita
Raj
raja
rani
rupee

s

samosa
sari
seersucker
shampoo
Sikh
sitar
swami

t

table
thug
toddy
tom-tom
topee

w

wallah

Persian

a

attar

b

baksheesh
bazaar

c

caravan
china

d

dervish

j

jackal
jasmine

k

kismet

l

lilac

m

Mogul
mummy
musk

p

pashmina
pistachio
pyjamas

s

scimitar
shah
shawl

t

taffeta
talc

Slavic languages

Most people living in Eastern Europe, the Balkans and
some parts of Asia speak a Slavic language. These include
Russian, Bulgarian, Polish, Czech, Croatian, Serbian,
Slovak, Bosnian, Macedonian, Ukrainian, Slovene and
Macedonian.

There has been some borrowing from these languages
into English, although it has been on a far smaller scale
than from other languages. It will be interesting to see if
the recent population movements from Eastern European

countries that have joined the European Union will have an effect on English.

Words from Slavic languages that are already established in English include:

Russian

a

agitprop

b

balalaika
beluga
Bolshevik
borscht
borzoi

c

Cossack

g

glasnost
Gulag

i

intelligentsia

k

kremlin

m

mammoth

p

perestroika
Politburo

r

rouble

s

samizdat
samovar
samoyed
shaman
soviet
sputnik
stroganoff

t

troika
tsar
tundra

v

vodka

Czech

howitzer
pistol

polka
robot

CHAPTER FIVE
Prefixes and Suffixes

Prefixes and suffixes can be added to words to make new words. If you are familiar with prefixes and suffixes and how they work in combination with other words, it will improve your spelling, your reading and your writing.

Prefixes

A prefix is a letter or group of letters that is added to the **beginning** of a word to make a new word.

A prefix can usually be attached to the front of another word without any change to the base word. Occasionally, a hyphen is inserted between the prefix and the word (for example, pro-democracy, pre-arranged) but this only happens with a few prefixes.

Prefix	Meaning	Examples
ab-	away from, not	abnormal, absolve, abscond, abstract, abhor
ad-	towards	address, addict, adjust, admit, advent, advise
al-	all	almost, always, altogether, although, already, almighty
ante-	before	antenatal, antecedent, anteroom, antediluvian
anti-	against	antiwar, anti-abortion, antidepressant, antisocial
auto-	self	autograph, automobile, autobiography, automatic
bi-	two or twice	bicycle, bimonthly, bifocal, bigamy, bicentenary
circum-	round or about	circumference, circulate, circle, circumstance
co-	together	cooperate, copilot, co-star, co-worker, co-write

Prefix	Meaning	Examples
col-	together	collateral, collaborate, collate, collide
com-	together	combine, combat, commit, compact, compare
con-	together	confer, condolence, constellation, converge
contra-	against	contraflow, contraception, contradict, contravene
cor-	together	correlation
de-	undo or remove	defrost, dethrone, deforest, decaffeinated, defuse
dis-	not	disease, disagree, dishonest, disinfect, dislodge, distrust
ex-	out or outside of	exit, explode, exterior, export, external
ex-	former	ex-husband, ex-wife, ex-president, ex-boss

Prefix	Meaning	Examples
il-	not	illegal, illegible, illegitimate, illiterate
im-	not	immobile, immoral, imperfect, imbalance, impossible
im-	in or into	immigrate, impregnate
in-	not	inhuman, insufferable, incredible, inexperience, indirect
in-	in or into	infiltrate, incite
inter-	between	international, intercept, interface, interrupt, interwar, interval
ir-	not	irregular, irrelevant, irreplaceable, irreverent
micro-	small	microscope, microchip, microcomputer, microfilm
mini-	small	miniskirt, miniature, minicomputer, minibus, minimum

Prefix	Meaning	Examples
mis-	wrong or false	misbehave, miscount, misfire, misinform, misfortune
non-	not	nonsmoking, nonfiction, nonstop, nonstick, nonsense
pre-	before	predate, pre-book, pre-arranged, pre-war, preseason
pro-	ahead or forward	propel, proactive, procreate, propose, protest
pro-	in favour of	pro-democracy, pro-Chinese, pro-choice, probiotic
re-	again	reread, remarriage, reoffend, repaint, reapply, reheat
sub-	under	submarine, subject, subordinate, subsoil, subway
sus-	under	suspect, suspend, sustain

Prefix	Meaning	Examples
tele-	distant	telegraph, telephone, television, telepathy, telescope
trans-	across	transfer, transmit, transplant, transatlantic, transport
ultra-	beyond or extremely	ultraviolet, ultramodern, ultravirus, ultrasound
un-	not	unhappy, undo, unlock, uncertainty, unused, unaware

FAQ . . .

What is the plural of 'roof'?

The plural of 'roof' is 'roofs', not to be confused with one plural form of 'hoof': 'hooves'.

Suffixes

A suffix is a letter or group of letters that is added to the **end** of a word to make a new word.

Some words change when a suffix is added. This change can depend on the letter at the end of the word and the letter at the beginning of the suffix. See the section called 'The spelling rules you really need to know' on pages 47-62 for the rules on adding suffixes. If a word ending and suffix combination is not mentioned there, you simply add the suffix to the end of the word without making any other change

Suffix	Meaning	Examples
-able	able to	breakable, readable, touchable, enjoyable, avoidable
-al	related to	medical, personal, seasonal, national, traditional
-ance	state or quality of	resemblance, attendance, acceptance, defiance, elegance

Suffix	Meaning	Examples
-ary	related to	cautionary, revolutionary, documentary, elementary, library
-ate	become or take on	hyphenate, medicate, elasticate, pollinate
-ation	action or state of	hospitalization, radicalization, legalization
-cian	profession of	physician, politician, mathematician, electrician, magician
-dom	state or condition of	freedom, boredom, martyrdom
-en	become	deepen, deaden, dampen, blacken, redden
-ence	state or quality of	benevolence, residence, patience, abstinence, dependence
-er	person from	Londoner, islander, Highlander, villager

Suffix	Meaning	Examples
-er	thing that does a job	fastener, lighter, scraper, trimmer, cutter
-er	person who does a job	reader, driver, baker, writer, painter, teacher
-er	more	cleverer, fatter, prettier, smellier, calmer, greener
-est	most	cleverest, fattest, prettiest, smelliest, calmest, greenest
-ette	small	kitchenette, cigarette, dinette, diskette, maisonette
-ful	full of	hopeful, successful, beautiful, pitiful, painful, resentful
-fy	make or become	beautify, notify, purify, clarify, citify, intensify
-hood	state of condition of	priesthood, childhood, manhood, likelihood, knighthood

Suffix	Meaning	Examples
-ible	able to	edible, reversible, possible, terrible, horrible
-ic	related to	metallic, atomic, organic, historic, rhythmic, periodic
-ication	action	notification, classification, clarification
-ion	action or state	election, prohibition, exhibition
-ish	fairly or rather	brownish, smallish, tigerish, youngish, boyish
-ism	action or condition	criticism, heroism, paganism, absenteeism, romanticism
-ism	prejudice	sexism, racism, anti-Semitism, ageism, heightism, weightism

Suffix	Meaning	Examples
-ist	of an action or condition	motorist, soloist, extremist, artist, novelist, machinist
-ist	prejudiced	sexist, racist, ageist, heightist, weightiest
-ition	action or state of	repetition, competition, opposition, position, petition
-ity	state or condition of	reality, continuity, stupidity, mobility, passivity
-ive	tending to	divisive, expensive, explosive, decorative, narrative, active
-ize	change or affect	radicalize, motorize, legalize, economize, hospitalize
-less	without	homeless, lifeless, speechless, endless, merciless, fearless

Suffix	Meaning	Examples
-like	resembling	baglike, doglike, doughlike, childlike, dreamlike, godlike
-ling	small	duckling, gosling, pigling, princeling
-ly	in this manner	kindly, friendly, personally, properly, really, weekly
-ment	state of having	contentment, resentment, enjoyment, employment
-ness	state or quality of	kindness, blindness, happiness, tenderness, selfishness
-ology	study or science of	biology, geology, archaeology, philology, musicology
-ship	state or condition of	fellowship, partnership, dictatorship, horsemanship

Suffix	Meaning	Examples
-sion	action or state of	confusion, decision, conclusion, explosion, supervision
-some	tending to	tiresome, awesome, quarrelsome, bothersome, troublesome
-tion	action or state of	creation, hibernation, relegation, production, calculation
-y	like or full of	sandy, hilly, grassy, watery, pebbly, snowy, milky

Double suffixes

Sometimes a suffix can have another suffix attached to it to make an even longer word. Some examples are shown here.

avail + **able** + **ity** = availability
commend + **able** + **ly** = commendably
accept + **able** + **ness** = acceptableness

emotion +**al** + **ism** = emotionalism

agriculture + **al** + **ist** = agriculturalist

nation + **al** + **ity** = nationality

person + **al** + **ly** = personally

natural + **al** + **ness** = naturalness

medic + **ate** + **ion** = medication

music + **cian** + **ship** = musicianship

damp + **en** + **er** = dampener

paint + **er** + **ly** = painterly

leader + **er** + **ship** = leadership

hope + **ful** + **ly** = hopefully

care + **ful** + **ness** = carefulness

access + **ible** + **ity** = accessibility

response + **ible** + **ly** = responsibly

in + access + **ible** + **ness** = inaccessibleness

history + **ic** + **al** = historical

confess + **ion** + **al** = confessional

extort + **ion** + **ist** = extortionist

contort + **ion** + **ism** = contortionism

girl + **ish** + **ly** = girlishly

amateur + **ish** + **ness** = amateurishness

add + **ition** + **al** = additional

oppose + **ition** + **ist** = oppositionist

expense + **ive** + **ly** =expensively

abuse + **ive** + **ness** = abusiveness

care + **less** + **ly** = carelessly

fear + **less** + **ness** = fearlessness

fertile + **ize** + **er** = fertilizer

friend + **ly** + **er** = friendlier

friend + **ly** + **est** = friendliest

kind + **ly** + **ness** = kindliness

astro + **ology** + **er** = astrologer

geo + **ology** + **ist** = geologist

awe + **some** + **ly** = awesomely

tire + **some** + **ness** = tiresomeness

intervene + **tion** + **ism** = interventionism

intervene + **tion** + **ist** = interventionist

grass + **y** + **er** = grassier

grass + **y** + **est** = grassiest

breeze + **y** + **ly** = breezily

air + **y** + **ness** = airiness

EXERCISE 4

PREFIXES

Prefixes go at the beginning of a word. There are many prefixes.

Here are some examples: **im-**, **in-**, **ir-**, **il-**, **mis-**, **non-**, **un-**, **anti-**, **bi-**, **co-**, **contra-**, **sub-**

You **add** a prefix to beginning of a word. Occasionally, you need a hyphen after the prefix, e.g. anti-inflationary.

1 Circle the prefixes.

inaccurate	immature	irregular	illegal
incapable	improper	irresponsible	illegible
indecent	impolite	irresistible	illiterate

misplace	nonsmoker	unhelpful	antibiotic
misread	nonstop	unlikely	anticlockwise
misfire	nonstick	unrealistic	anticlimax

EXERCISE 4

2 What do you think are the meanings of these prefixes?

in _____

im _____

ir _____

il _____

mis _____

non _____

un _____

anti _____

EXERCISE 4

3 Change the meaning of these sentences by adding a prefix.

e.g.   The handwriting is legible.
The handwriting is illegible.

(a) Turn the handle clockwise.

(b) I am quite capable of doing that!

(c) I have placed my glasses somewhere.

(d) That girl is very mature.

(e) Is it legal to park here?

EXERCISE 4

CONSONANT SUFFIXES

Adding **consonant suffixes**, such as **-s, -ness, -ly, -hood, -ship, -dom, -ment, -like** and **less** is usually straightforward. Simply **add** the suffix to the base word.

e.g. help + less = helpless

When adding **-ful** (to be full of something), make sure you only have a single **l** at the end.

Be careful: beauty + ful = beautiful

This also applies to mercy, fancy, bounty, pity and plenty.

Hints & Tips . . .

Different people learn spelling in different ways. Find out how you learn best.

EXERCISE 4

4 Match each word to a consonant suffix.

hope	ment
child	ness
enjoy	ship
mad	ly
friend	like
king	ful
sudden	dom
wonder	less

5 Write a word within a sentence using each of these consonant suffixes.

hood   ship   ness   less   like

EXERCISE 4

VOWEL SUFFIXES

Examples of **vowel suffixes** are: **-ed**, **-ing**, **-es** and **-ed**. Adding vowel suffixes needs more care.

Be careful: You need to look at the ending of the base word. Does it end with a vowel, a consonant or **y**?
Decide whether to **add**, **drop e**, **double** or **change y**.

See the section called 'The spelling rules you really need to know' on pages 47–62 and the 'Suffixes' section on pages 131–140 for more on adding vowel suffixes.

6 Complete these sentences by adding the correct suffix. At the end of each sentence, write the rule you have used.

e.g. I am include + *ing* John on the list. (Rule: *drop e*)

(a) He carry _____ the shopping all the way to his flat. (Rule: _____)

EXERCISE 4

(b) We were chuckle _____ about the joke on

the TV. (Rule: _____)

(c) Alice was dream _____ about the holiday

she would have. (Rule: _____)

(d) Wayne has been drop _____ from the

football team. (Rule: _____)

(e) He was hope _____ to get a Saturday job in

the High Street. (Rule: _____)

(f) Dad was strip _____ the wallpaper from the

kitchen wall. (Rule: _____)

(g) "I'm not doing that!" I reply _____ quickly.

(Rule: _____)

EXERCISE 4

(h) The frost disappear _____ from the grass as soon as the sun came out. (Rule: _____)

(i) The evidence was bury _____ in the ground. (Rule: _____)

7 Complete the table by identifying the prefixes and suffixes in these words.

	Prefix	Base word	Suffix
irreplaceable			
irremovable			
insincerely			
uncomfortable			
impossibility			
unhappiness			
antiheroes			
miscommunication			

CHAPTER SIX
Further Building Blocks in Spelling

English has many words that contain Greek and Latin roots. Some of these roots appear in lots of different words, and are still used regularly to create new words. If you can get to know these roots, how to spell them and what they mean, you will find it a great help in your reading and writing, as well as in your spelling.

aero

Aero comes from Greek *aēr* meaning 'air'. The word **aero** is used as an abbreviation for aircraft or aeronautics; it is also the name of a chocolate bar promoted for its bubbly lightness.

Examples

aeroplane	aeronautics	aerate
aerobics	aerosol	anaerobic
aerodrome	aerospace	
aerodynamics	aerial	

ambi

Ambi comes from Latin *ambo* meaning 'both'.

Examples

ambidextrous	ambisexual
ambivalent	

anthrop

Anthrop comes from Greek *anthrōpos* meaning 'human'

Examples

anthropology	anthropoid
anthropomorphic	misanthrope
anthropocentric	philanthropist
anthropophagus	lycanthrope

aqua

Aqua is the Latin word for 'water'.

Examples

aqualung	aquarium	subaqua
aquamarine	Aquarius	
aquatic	aquaerobics	

Sometimes the second **a** changes to another vowel.

Examples

aqueduct	aquiculture	subaqueous
aqueous	aquifer	

astro

Astro comes from Greek *astron* meaning 'star'.

Examples

astronomy	astronaut	astrotourist
astrology	astrophysics	
astrochemistry	astrolabe	

audi

Audi comes from Latin *audīre* meaning 'to hear'.

Examples

audible	audiotypist	auditorium
audience	audiovisual	auditory
audio	audit	inaudible
audiology	audition	

bio

Bio comes from Greek *bios* meaning 'life'.

Examples

biology	biography	biotechnology
biochemistry	biometric	autobiography
biodiversity	biopsy	antibiotic
biodegradable	bio-organism	probiotic

cede

Cede comes from Latin *cēdere* meaning 'to yield'.

Examples

cede	concede	secede
accede	precede	recede

cent

Cent comes from Latin *centum* meaning 'hundred'. **Cent** is a monetary unit in many countries, taking its name from the fact that it is worth one hundredth of the main unit of currency: for example, a **cent** is one hundredth of the American dollar and the euro.

Examples

century	centigrade	centipede
centenary	centimetre	per cent
centenarian	centilitre	percentage

clude

Clude comes from Latin *claudere* meaning 'to close'.

Examples

conclude	include	preclude
exclude	occlude	seclude

cred

Cred comes from Latin *crēdere* meaning 'to believe'. **Cred** is used as an informal shortened form of **credibility**, especially in the phrase 'street credibility'.

Examples

credible	credo	accredit
credence	credulous	discredit
credenza	credential	incredible
credit	creditable	incredulous

Hints & Tips . . .

Be careful not to confuse the spelling *aer* with *air*. Remember it's **aer**oplane, but **air**port.

cycle

Cycle comes from Late Latin *cyclus*, which is itself derived from Greek *kuklos* meaning 'cycle', 'circle', 'wheel' or 'ring'. The second **e** changes to another vowel when it is used as a prefix. When it appears as the first part of a word, the **y** is pronounced 'ai' (as in 'tie') rather than 'i' (as in 'sit') – although **cyclic** and **cyclical** can be said either way. When it appears in the middle or at the end of a word, the pronunciation of the **y** depends on where the word is stressed. But no matter how it is pronounced, it is always spelt 'cycl'.

Examples

cycle	cyclone	tricycle
cyclic	encyclical	unicycle
cyclical	epicycle	motorcycle
cyclorama	recycle	
Cyclops	bicycle	

duo

Duo is Latin for 'two'.

Examples

duo	duodecimal	duet
duologue	duodenum	
duopoly	duodenal	

geo

Geo comes from Greek *gē* meaning 'earth'.

Examples

geology	geode	geothermal
geography	geophysics	biogeography
geometry	geopolitics	zoogeography

graph

Graph comes from Greek *graphein* meaning 'to write'.

Examples

graph	choreographer	monograph
graphic	chronograph	phonograph
graphite	digraph	pictograph
graphology	electrocardiograph	polygraph
autograph	epigraph	telegraph
photograph	holograph	
paragraph	lithographer	

hydro

Hydro comes from Greek *hudōr* meaning 'water'. **Hydro** is used as a shortened form of **hydroelectric**. A **hydro** is also a hotel or resort that offers **hydropathy**, which is the treatment of disease using large quantities of water internally and externally. Although this medical treatment has been discredited and is no longer practised, some hotels retain the name **hydro**. It is interesting to see that both the Greek and the Latin words for 'water' are productive root words in English.

Examples

hydrocarbon	hydrotherapy	anhydride
hydrocephalus	hydroxyl	anhydrous
hydrochloric	hydra	carbohydrate
hydrofoil	hydracids	dehydrogenate
hydrogen	hydrangea	dehydrate
hydrolysis	hydrant	rehydrate
hydrophobia	hydrate	
hydroplane	hydraulic	

nova

Nova comes from Latin *novus* meaning 'new'. The **a** changes to another vowel when it is used as a prefix. When used as a prefix, the **o** is said the same as the vowel in 'dog'. When it is on its own or at the end of a word, the **o** is the same as that in 'know'. When the **o** is in the middle of the word (as in **renovate** and **innovate**), it has the same unstressed vowel sound that comes at the end of 'melon'.

Examples

nova	novelty	renovate
novel	novice	supernova
novella	innovate	

oct

Oct comes from Latin *octō* meaning 'eight': the Greek word is *oktō*.

Examples

octagon	octillion	octopus
octave	octant	octoroon
octet	octennial	octuple
octavo	October	
octahedron	octogenarian	

paed

Paed or paedo comes from Greek *pais* meaning 'child'. The American spellings are 'ped' and 'pedo'. In British English it is pronounced to rhyme with 'seed'. However, in America and Australia it rhymes with 'said'.

Examples

paediatrics	paediatrician	paedophile

ped

Ped comes from Latin *pēs* meaning 'foot'. It is always pronounced as it is written, to rhyme with 'said'. Do not confuse it with the American spelling of 'paed', which sometimes has the same pronunciation.

Examples

pedal	pedicure	biped
pedestrian	pedometer	quadruped

philia

Philia comes from Greek philos meaning 'loving'. 'Phile' is pronounced as 'file', while all other occurrences of 'phil' are pronounced 'fill', no matter what letter follows it.

Examples

philanthropy	philodendron	bibliophile
philander	Philadelphia	paedophile
philately	philosophy	Francophile
philology	haemophilia	cinephile
philharmonic	haemophiliac	

phobia

Phobia comes from Greek *phobos* meaning 'fear'. It appears in hundreds of words relating to the fear or hatred of certain people, animals, objects, situations and activities.

Examples

phobia	agoraphobia	xenophobe
phobic	agoraphobic	homophobia
claustrophobia	xenophobia	homophobic
claustrophobic	xenophobic	Anglophobia

phono

Phono or phon comes from Greek *phōnē* meaning 'sound' or 'voice'. 'Phone' at the end of a word rhymes with 'moan'. The **o** in 'phonic' has the same vowel sound as that in 'dog'. 'Phon' in **phoneme**, **phonograph** and **euphonium** has the same pronunciation as 'phone'. In **phonetic**, **cacophony**, **symphony** and **telephony**, 'phon' has the same unstressed vowel sound that comes at the end of 'melon'.

Examples

phone	quadraphonic	microphone
phoneme	stereophonic	saxophone
phonetic	telephone	xylophone
phonics	headphone	cacophony
phonograph	homophone	symphony
phonology	earphone	telephony
euphonium	megaphone	
polyphonic	gramophone	

photo

Photo comes from Greek *phōs* meaning 'light'.

Examples

photo	Photofit	photosynthesis
photograph	photocell	telephoto
photocopier	photolysis	
photoelectric	photosensitive	

poly

Poly comes from Greek *polus* meaning 'many' or 'much'. The word **poly** is used as an abbreviation for **polytechnic**, **polyester** and **polythene**.

Examples

polygamy	polyhedron	polysemy
polyester	polygraph	polystyrene
polythene	polymath	polytheism
polyanthus	polymorph	polypeptide
polytechnic	polynomial	Polynesia
polygon	polyphonic	polyp

port

Port comes from Latin *portāre* meaning 'to carry'.

Examples

porter	teleport	purport
portable	comportment	report
portmanteau	import	rapport
portfolio	export	support
transport	deport	

prim

Prim comes from Latin *prīmus* meaning 'first'. The 'prim' syllable in **primitive**, **primrose** and **primula** rhymes with 'dim'. In the other words it rhymes with 'time'.

Examples

primary	primetime	primordial
primate	primal	primogeniture
prime	primeval	primrose
primer	primitive	primula

scope

Scope comes from Greek *skopein* meaning 'to look at'. When the word ends in scope, it rhymes with 'hope'. In all other circumstances 'scop' rhymes with 'stop'.

Examples

microscope	horoscope	endoscopic
telescope	oscilloscope	microscopic
periscope	stethoscope	kaleidoscopic
endoscope	bioscope	
kaleidoscope	endoscopy	

scribe

Scribe comes from Latin *scrībere* meaning 'to write'. When the suffix **-tion** is added to make a noun from a verb ending in 'scribe', the **e** is dropped and the **b** becomes **p**, as in **description**, **subscription**, **prescription** and **inscription**.

Examples

scribe	circumscribe	proscribe
scriber	describe	subscribe
scribble	inscribe	transcribe
ascribe	prescribe	unsubscribe

tri

Tri comes from Latin *trēs* meaning 'three': the Greek word is *treis*. In most words 'tri' is pronounced like 'try'. In others it has the vowel sound of 'trip'. In **trio**, it is pronounced like 'tree'.

Examples

triangle	tricolour	trinity
trio	tricorn	tripod
triad	tricycle	triplicate
Triassic	triennial	triptych
triathlon	trilateral	trireme
tricentenary	trilingual	trisect
triceps	trilogy	trivalent

vis

Vis comes from Latin *vīsus* meaning 'sight' which itself comes from *vidēre* meaning 'to see'.

Examples

visual	visit	supervise
visible	vista	televise
vision	revise	television

FAQ . . .

Which is correct: licence or license?
An easy way to remember the difference is that 'licence' is the noun and 'license' is the verb. Try using these sayings to help you remember:

I want to see (c) your licence
the government licenses schnapps

EXERCISE 5

1 Below are ten root words. Can you use them to make words?

Draw a line to join each of the root words with a word beginning or ending from the panel on the right.

Root words

astro	claustro
bio	copy
cent	naut
duo	ury
graph	ible
oct	agon
phobia	micro
photo	graphy
scope	photo
vis	denum

EXERCISE 5

2 Look up the following words in your dictionary.

Write a definition for each and then try to put the word into a sentence.

aero means
_____

aerodrome   *small airport*   *The private plane*
landed at the
aerodrome.

aerodynamic _____

_____

_____

aeroplane _____

_____

_____

EXERCISE 5

aqua means

_____

aquarium _____

_____

_____

aquatic _____

_____

_____

aqueduct _____

_____

_____

EXERCISE 5

audi means

_____

audible _____

_____

_____

audience _____

_____

_____

audition _____

_____

_____

EXERCISE 5

geo means

_____

geology _____

_____

_____

geography _____

_____

_____

geometry _____

_____

_____

EXERCISE 5

ped means

_____

pedal _____

_____

_____

pedestrian _____

_____

_____

quadruped _____

_____

_____

EXERCISE 5

scope means

_____

microscope _____

_____

_____

telescope _____

_____

_____

stethoscope _____

_____

_____

EXERCISE 5

tri means _____

triangle _____

_____

_____

triathlon _____

_____

_____

trilogy _____

_____

_____

PUZZLES

One Too Many

tommorrow

rhinosceros

sandwitch

seaparate

quiery

dissappeared

luxuryious

suggar

neccessary

innoculate

☐ ☐ ☐ ☐ ☐ ☐ ☐ ☐ ☐ ☐

— — — — — — — — — —

Each word has ONE letter too many.
Cross out the extra letters and put them in the small boxes.

JUMBLE THESE TO MAKE ... A SPORT!

1 Missing

clarvoyant

sopisticated

spontaneus

Parliment

idylic

labrinth

stradled

One letter is missing in each word. Write each missing letter in the 7 circles below

◯◯◯◯◯◯◯ = __ __ __ __ __ __ __

Jumble these to make another word! | clue: time off!

---

symetrical

terestrial

Mediteranean

ubiquitus

vetrinary

sking

embeded

underated

Try the same again... this time making an 8 letter word

| clue: on reflection!

◯◯◯◯◯◯◯◯ = __ __ __ __ __ __ __ __

Tricky Eights!

- Cross out the incorrect spelling of each of the 12 words!
- Find all the correct words in the word search! (none diagonal)
- Look and cover 3 words at a time and give yourself a spelling test!

separate seperate	accident acsident	commense commence
definate definite	nuisance nuisanse	humourus humorous
spatious spacious	brochure broshure	bootique boutique
sanwitch sandwich	electric elektric	thorough thurough

```
S X E Y E C N E M M O C
E H T A D E S F G M O P
P G I J A M P M T Z S Q
A U N U I S A N C E U S
R O I E S Z C Q R R O A
A R F M O Q I N F U R N
T O E N J R O G H H O D
E H D X Z Y U I A C M W
V T U Z T M S X B O U I
W B O U T I Q U E R H C
E L E C T R I C C B O H
T N E D I C C A M N P R
```

1. _____
2. _____
3. _____
4. _____
5. _____
6. _____
7. _____
8. _____
9. _____
10. _____
11. _____
12. _____

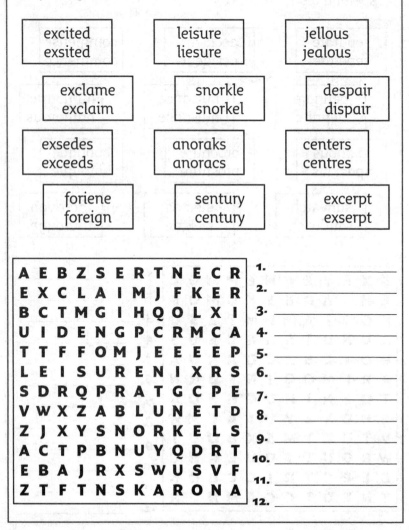

Tricky Sevens!

- Cross out the incorrect spelling of each of the 12 words!
- Find all the correct words in the word search! (none diagonal)
- Look and cover 3 words at a time and give yourself a spelling test!

excited exsited	leisure liesure	jellous jealous
exclame exclaim	snorkle snorkel	despair dispair
exsedes exceeds	anoraks anoracs	centers centres
foriene foreign	sentury century	excerpt exserpt

```
A E B Z S E R T N E C R
E X C L A I M J F K E R
B C T M G I H Q O L X I
U I D E N G P C R M C A
T T F F O M J E E E E P
L E I S U R E N I X R S
S D R Q P R A T G C P E
V W X Z A B L U N E T D
Z J X Y S N O R K E L S
A C T P B N U Y Q D R T
E B A J R X S W U S V F
Z T F T N S K A R O N A
```

1. _____
2. _____
3. _____
4. _____
5. _____
6. _____
7. _____
8. _____
9. _____
10. _____
11. _____
12. _____

176

One In Four

temprature	G
tempachure	J
temperature	A
temperture	Y

paralell	L
parallel	N
paralel	F
parralel	Z

millionaire	H
milionair	B
millionair	E
milionaire	T

rhythm	I
rithum	K
rithem	X
rhythem	L

gellusy	M
jealusy	O
gelousy	B
jealousy	C

hijean	P
hygiene	W
hyjean	V
higene	O

pygion	Q
pijeon	E
pygon	U
pigeon	D

xilophone	R
xylophone	S
zilophone	T
zylophone	E

◯ ◯ ◯ ◯ ◯ ◯ ◯ ◯

__ __ __ __ __ __ __ __

In each box choose the correct spelling.
Next to each correct spelling is a letter of the
  alphabet.
Put these letters in the 8 circles.
Jumble to make a word … for a quick snack!

At The Zoo

Use a pencil to correct all the spelling mistakes in the following passage and then rewrite it without an error to be seen!

The jurney to the zoo last Wensday was a grate sucess, exsept for me having an arguement with my best freind. You'll never beleive what about! The filings in our sanwiches! Still, when we got their we were best mates agen!

It's a good job to, otherwise we wouldn't have enjoyed the animals. We saw some beatiful girrafes and there neigbours, the fasinating gorrillas with there eenormus mussles. My favorites were the artic foxs, the spoted leperds and the miniture horses.

We had dinner in a lovly restrant althogh the vegtables were a bit under cooked espeshly the potatos! However, the vanila ice-scream was delishus. During the afternoon I was disapointed becuse the temprature dropped and their was an autum storm. Lightening flashed and it realy porred down so we shelterd. The rain soon stopped thogh, but it was nealy as cold as febuary!

Still, it was an exsellant day witch I will never forget egsept for the stomack ake I had threw eating one of my best frend's samwitches!

At The Zoo

1 Missing

acheve

brocoli

anesthetic

veicle

enviroment

facinated

disapointed

One letter is missing in each word. Write each missing letter in the 7 circles below

◯◯◯◯◯◯◯ = __ __ __ __ __ __ __

Jumble these to make another word!

clue: grub greenery!

---

gorgous

analsis

magarine

Caribean

miniture

embarass

cofee

camoflage

Try the same again... this time making an 8 letter word!

◯◯◯◯◯◯◯◯

clue: a month

__ __ __ __ __ __ __ __

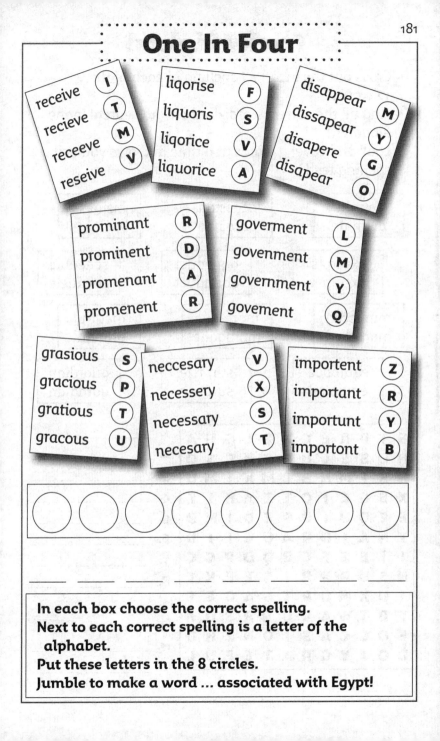

One In Four

Spelling	Letter
receive	I
recieve	T
receeve	M
reseive	V

Spelling	Letter
liqorise	F
liquoris	S
liqorice	V
liquorice	A

Spelling	Letter
disappear	M
dissapear	Y
disapere	G
disapear	O

Spelling	Letter
prominant	R
prominent	D
promenant	A
promenent	R

Spelling	Letter
goverment	L
govenment	M
government	Y
govement	Q

Spelling	Letter
grasious	S
gracious	P
gratious	T
gracous	U

Spelling	Letter
neccesary	V
necessery	X
necessary	S
necesary	T

Spelling	Letter
importent	Z
important	R
importunt	Y
importont	B

( ) ( ) ( ) ( ) ( ) ( ) ( ) ( )

In each box choose the correct spelling.
Next to each correct spelling is a letter of the
  alphabet.
Put these letters in the 8 circles.
Jumble to make a word … associated with Egypt!

Tricky Eights!

- Cross out the incorrect spelling of each of the 12 words!
- Find all the correct words in the word search! (none diagonal)
- Look and cover 3 words at a time and give yourself a spelling test!

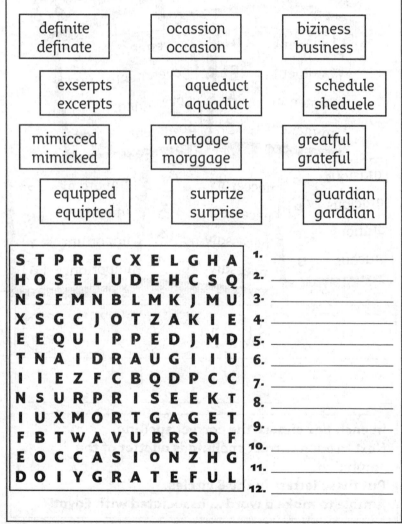

| definite | ocassion | biziness |
| definate | occasion | business |

| exserpts | aqueduct | schedule |
| excerpts | aquaduct | sheduele |

| mimicced | mortgage | greatful |
| mimicked | morggage | grateful |

| equipped | surprize | guardian |
| equipted | surprise | garddian |

```
S T P R E C X E L G H A
H O S E L U D E H C S Q
N S F M N B L M K J M U
X S G C J O T Z A K I E
E E Q U I P P E D J M D
T N A I D R A U G I I U
I I E Z F C B Q D P C C
N S U R P R I S E E K T
I U X M O R T G A G E T
F B T W A V U B R S D F
E O C C A S I O N Z H G
D O I Y G R A T E F U L
```

1. _____
2. _____
3. _____
4. _____
5. _____
6. _____
7. _____
8. _____
9. _____
10. _____
11. _____
12. _____

Endings -or/-er/-ar

Fill in the endings of these words. They end with either **-or**, **-er**, or **-ar**

Use your dictionary to check!

act ☐☐   popul ☐☐   doll ☐☐
badg ☐☐   chapt ☐☐   sail ☐☐
coll ☐☐   doct ☐☐   dang ☐☐
fath ☐☐   juni ☐☐   caterpill ☐☐
mirr ☐☐   regul ☐☐   visit ☐☐
vineg ☐☐   moth ☐☐   teach ☐☐

Memory and Spelling Test!

Now cover the lists and fill in 6 words for each notepad

-er
1. _____
2. _____
3. _____
4. _____
5. _____
6. _____

-or
1. _____
2. _____
3. _____
4. _____
5. _____
6. _____

-ar
1. _____
2. _____
3. _____
4. _____
5. _____
6. _____

Tricky Nines!

- Cross out the incorrect spelling of each of the 12 words!
- Find all the correct words in the word search! (none diagonal)
- Look and cover 3 words at a time and give yourself a spelling test!

| permenant permanent | hypocrisy hypocricy | guarentee guarantee |

| jewellery jewellary | faceteous facetious | advertise advertize |

| itinerary itinarary | dissapear disappear | miniscule minuscule |

| manuoevre manoeuvre | necessary neccesary | consensus concensus |

```
M E W T N E N A M R E P
A L D I S A P P E A R H
N U Y R A R E N I T I Y
O C O N S E N S U S G P
E S F L V D E M X K U O
U U C Q B O A A R M A C
V N X R F N P D J R R R
R I E S I T R E V D A I
E M S T F U T E I W N S
G J E W E L L E R Y T Y
Z S U O I T E C A F E Z
L Q V Y R A S S E C E N
```

1. _____
2. _____
3. _____
4. _____
5. _____
6. _____
7. _____
8. _____
9. _____
10. _____
11. _____
12. _____

Endings -a/-our/-re

Fill in the endings of these words with 1, 2, or 3 letters **-a**, **-re**, or **-our**

Use your dictionary to check!

arom☐☐☐　　ac☐☐☐　　sultan☐☐☐

glam☐☐☐　　aren☐☐☐　　vap☐☐☐

sab☐☐☐　　lab☐☐☐　　quot☐☐☐

met☐☐☐　　hum☐☐☐　　lust☐☐☐

hon☐☐☐　　mit☐☐☐　　meag☐☐☐

orchestr☐☐☐　　pand☐☐☐　　fav☐☐☐

Memory and Spelling Test!

Now cover the lists and fill in 6 words for each notepad

-re
1. _____
2. _____
3. _____
4. _____
5. _____
6. _____

-a
1. _____
2. _____
3. _____
4. _____
5. _____
6. _____

-our
1. _____
2. _____
3. _____
4. _____
5. _____
6. _____

Endings -a/-our/-re

Fill in the endings of these words with 1, 2, or 3 letters **-a**, **-re**, or **-our**

Use your dictionary to check!

banan ☐☐☐ rum ☐☐☐ neighb ☐☐☐

col ☐☐☐ lit ☐☐☐ millimet ☐☐☐

cent ☐☐☐ camer ☐☐☐ larv ☐☐☐

fib ☐☐☐ arm ☐☐☐ kilomet ☐☐☐

flav ☐☐☐ centimet ☐☐☐ harb ☐☐☐

zebr ☐☐☐ ide ☐☐☐ vanill ☐☐☐

Memory and Spelling Test!

Now cover the lists and fill in 6 words for each notepad

-a
1. _____
2. _____
3. _____
4. _____
5. _____
6. _____

-re
1. _____
2. _____
3. _____
4. _____
5. _____
6. _____

-our
1. _____
2. _____
3. _____
4. _____
5. _____
6. _____

One Too Many!

priviledge

separrate

humourous

dennial

disasterous

mischievious

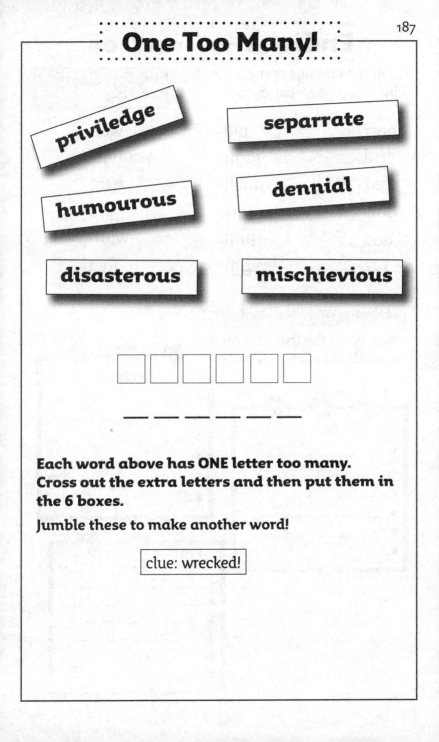

☐ ☐ ☐ ☐ ☐ ☐

___ ___ ___ ___ ___ ___

**Each word above has ONE letter too many.
Cross out the extra letters and then put them in
the 6 boxes.**

Jumble these to make another word!

clue: wrecked!

Endings -or/-ar/-er

Fill in the endings of these words with either **-or**, **-ar**, or **-er**

Use your dictionary to check!

horr ☐☐   pill ☐☐   wait ☐☐
rul ☐☐   jagu ☐☐   youngst ☐☐
ced ☐☐   anch ☐☐   nect ☐☐
guit ☐☐   bak ☐☐   pol ☐☐
add ☐☐   equat ☐☐   warri ☐☐
raz ☐☐   daught ☐☐   fact ☐☐

Memory and Spelling Test!

Now cover the lists and fill in 6 words for each notepad

-ar
1. _____
2. _____
3. _____
4. _____
5. _____
6. _____

-or
1. _____
2. _____
3. _____
4. _____
5. _____
6. _____

-er
1. _____
2. _____
3. _____
4. _____
5. _____
6. _____

Tricky Sevens!

- Cross out the incorrect spelling of each of the 12 words!
- Find all the correct words in the word search! (none diagonal)
- Look and cover 3 words at a time and give yourself a spelling test!

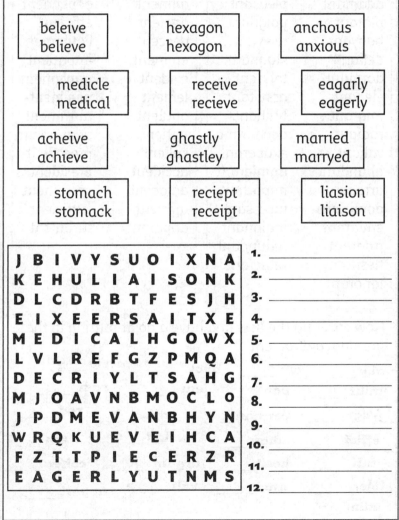

| beleive | hexagon | anchous |
| believe | hexogon | anxious |

| medicle | receive | eagarly |
| medical | recieve | eagerly |

| acheive | ghastly | married |
| achieve | ghastley | marryed |

| stomach | reciept | liasion |
| stomack | receipt | liaison |

```
J B I V Y S U O I X N A
K E H U L I A I S O N K
D L C D R B T F E S J H
E I X E E R S A I T X E
M E D I C A L H G O W X
L V L R E F G Z P M Q A
D E C R I Y L T S A H G
M J O A V N B M O C L O
J P D M E V A N B H Y N
W R Q K U E V E I H C A
F Z T T P I E C E R Z R
E A G E R L Y U T N M S
```

1. _____
2. _____
3. _____
4. _____
5. _____
6. _____
7. _____
8. _____
9. _____
10. _____
11. _____
12. _____

-ant or -ent?

Easily confused? Look at the lists — then look up any words you don't know in your dictionary

mutant	irritant	absent	argument
tenant	militant	parent	coherent
vacant	occupant	rodent	deficient
adamant	pleasant	ailment	dependent
blatant	poignant	ancient	efficient
buoyant	relevant	descent	equipment
defiant	stagnant	eminent	impatient
dormant	tolerant	evident	implement
elegant	assistant	lenient	negligent
migrant	brilliant	opulent	nutriment
radiant	deodorant	patient	permanent
valiant	exuberant	salient	precedent
abundant	immigrant	accident	president
arrogant	important	adjacent	prominent
dominant	incessant	affluent	sufficient
emigrant	indignant	apparent	turbulent
fragrant	redundant		
hesitant	reluctant		
ignorant			

Now cover up the lists and have a go at putting in the missing 'ant' or 'ent'

abs _____   vac _____   buoy _____   accid _____

milit _____   par _____   leni _____   radi _____

fragr _____   perman _____   adjac _____   rod _____

effici _____   indign _____   poign _____   ten _____

sali _____   hesit _____   argum _____   coher _____

toler _____   anci _____   vali _____   appar _____

ailm _____

-able or -ible?

Easily confused? Look at the lists — then look up any words you don't know in your dictionary

amiable	suitable	audible	possible
capable	adaptable	legible	sensible
durable	admirable	risible	tangible
lovable	advisable	visible	terrible
movable	agreeable	credible	divisible
notable	allowable	eligible	illegible
pliable	available	flexible	inaudible
adorable	debatable	gullible	indelible
amenable	desirable	horrible	invisible
amicable	enjoyable	inedible	plausible
arguable	excitable		
culpable	flammable		
enviable	habitable		
probable	incapable		
reliable	irritable		
reusable	palatable		
sociable	tolerable		

Now cover up the lists and have a go at putting in the missing 'a's or 'i's below

cap _ ble	gull _ ble	leg _ ble	desir _ ble
ami _ ble	prob _ ble	incap _ ble	divis _ ble
plaus _ ble	incred _ ble	reus _ ble	terr _ ble
tang _ ble	advis _ ble	flamm _ ble	elig _ ble
vis _ ble	ador _ ble	culp _ ble	sens _ ble
inaud _ ble	pli _ ble	poss _ ble	irrit _ ble
ris _ ble	dur _ ble	indel _ ble	debat _ ble

Down Town

Use a pencil to correct all the spelling mistakes in the following passage and then rewrite it without an error to be seen!

It was a misrable saterday morning in janruary. Becus I was a bit board i disided i fancyed a walk into town. I set of about ten oclock and fistly hedded doen are avinoo. I past the locle libary, are skool and then wonderd threw the disserted park towards the town senter.

It began to drizzel and then it proply pored down! I got reely sokked! Luckly it stopt after about a qurter of an our. At eggsactly midday I past the fire-stayshun and to my grate serprize, a fire-enjun shot out and neely flatend me!

It must of bin doing eigty miles-an-our! At leest!

After I recuverd and coat my breth, i kwikly maid for the jigantik shopin senter. I felt a bit peckish so i had a snak and a cofee in a litel caffy next door to my favrit moosic storr.

Then i met one of my mates, micheal.

I was shokkt to here his noos!

He tolled me all about is cat being stuk up there sickamor tree, just dow are avinoo!

"Ah! Thats were the fire-enjun was speedin too!" i wreckond.

Enyway, to cut a long storey short, micheal invyted me to is plaice, and we spent the wrest of the aternoon playing compewter games in is room, with his reskewed jinga cat for kumpani.

I must say that it lookt aa tutch shacken and nurvus!

Mind you, you'd be a bit jumpie avin bin stuk up a tree all morning! Wood'nt you?

Down Town

Quiz Quest!

Can you complete these words which all contain '**qu**' ... and join them to their definitions?

t _ _ _ _ oise

_ _ _ irr _ _

ob _ _ _ _ _

mo _ _ _ _ _ o

fr _ _ _ _ _ tly

bo _ _ _ _ t

bo _ _ iq _ _

a _ _ qu _ _ _

squ _ _ _ _ _

un _ _ _ _

b _ _ qu _ _

el _ _ _ ent

squ _ _ _ _ _ _

_ _ _ i _ _ _

_ pa _ _ _

equ _ _ _ _ _ _ _

ubi _ _ _ _ _ _

_ _ _ tur _ _ _ _ _

- enough
- a great feast
- a bunch of flowers
- to speak or write with ease
- a valuable item from the past
- often
- to waste
- cannot be seen through
- a blood sucking insect
- a bluish-green colour
- something which seems to be everywhere at the same time
- a place that is attractive and unspoiled
- a line sloping at an angle
- easily upset by unpleasant sights
- relating to or involving horses
- a woodland creature
- being the only one of its kind
- a small shop selling fashionable clothes

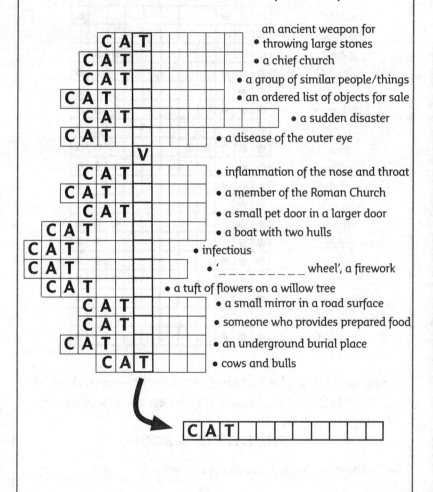

Starters ...

All the answers to the clues begin with the same 3 letters. Fill in the missing letters to reveal another clue down the ladder. Answer this to complete the puzzle.

C A T • an ancient weapon for throwing large stones

C A T • a chief church

C A T • a group of similar people/things

C A T • an ordered list of objects for sale

C A T • a sudden disaster

C A T • a disease of the outer eye

V

C A T • inflammation of the nose and throat

C A T • a member of the Roman Church

C A T • a small pet door in a larger door

C A T • a boat with two hulls

C A T • infectious

C A T • '_ _ _ _ _ _ _ _ _ wheel', a firework

C A T • a tuft of flowers on a willow tree

C A T • a small mirror in a road surface

C A T • someone who provides prepared food

C A T • an underground burial place

C A T • cows and bulls

C A T

Ladder Spell!

visiter
dissapoint
sugest
alowed
bilding
colum
disiner
nee
safty
hellthy
sincerly
auther
girafe
memery
atemt
arkitekt
thermomeeter
conseel

Each word is spelled wrongly – correct them and write the words in the grid opposite. When complete, down the ladder will be:

THE TITLE OF A BOOK!

• Try covering the grid and giving yourself a spelling test!

One In Four

sensable **J**
sensible **O**
sencible **Z**
censible **B**

dismisle **F**
dissmisle **T**
dismissel **O**
dismissal **L**

fraze **K**
phraise **B**
phrase **E**
fraize **J**

fawlty **A**
fallty **C**
faulty **E**
faltey **B**

recommend **V**
recomened **D**
reccomend **F**
recomend **M**

playright **Q**
playwright **P**
playwrite **Y**
playrite **I**

puntuation **K**
punkuation **X**
punctation **S**
punctuation **N**

associate **E**
asosiate **T**
assosiate **G**
ascociate **R**

◯ ◯ ◯ ◯ ◯ ◯ ◯ ◯

In each box choose the correct spelling.
Next to each correct spelling is a letter of the alphabet.
Put these letters in the 8 circles.
Jumble to make a word ... A STATIONERY ITEM!

Phantastic Phantoms

Can you complete these words, which all contain 'ph' ... and join them to their definitions?

au _ _ _ ra _ _ •   • ghost

_ le _ _ a _ t   • bird

geo _ _ _ _ _ y   • chemist shop

meg _ _ _ _ _ e   • school subject

mic _ _ _ _ one   • signature

n _ _ _ _ w   • group of sentences

ph _ _ _ om   • relative

ph _ _ _ a _ y   • musical instrument

_ _ eas _ _ _   • for magnifying a voice

_ _ ot _ g _ _ _ _   • large mammal

s _ x _ p _ _ _ _   • remembrance stone

sp _ _ _ x   • in a pop singer's hand

p _ _ ag _ _ _ _   • taken by a camera

ce _ _ t _ _ _   • Egyptian statue

Ladder Spell!

▼

suprise										
releif										
anceint										
vinigar										
samon										
reciept										
supose										
jellus										
freindly										
fataly										
gastly										
conciet										
burgler										
seeze										
parralel										
visiter										
knifes										
exersize										

Each word is spelled wrongly – correct them and write the words in the grid opposite. When complete, down the ladder will be:

TWO FRUITS

1 Missing

sovreign

mischievus

millenium

posession

inocuous

tomorro

comitment

One letter is missing in each word. Write each missing letter in the 7 circles below

◯◯◯◯◯◯◯ = __ __ __ __ __ __ __

Jumble these to make another word! | clue: cool guys!

---

goverment

vicinty

sychology

consience

lothe

puntual

disapear

behavior

choclate

instint

Try the same again... this time making a 10 letter word

clue: hot drink!

◯◯◯◯◯◯◯◯◯◯

__ __ __ __ __ __ __ __ __ __

Singles or Doubles?

Can you complete these words and join them to their definitions?

In the boxes, decide whether you want a single letter or a double.

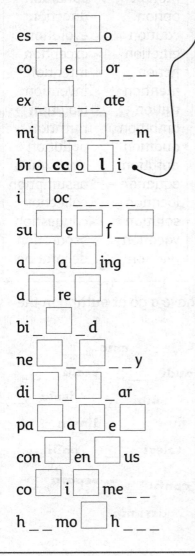

es ___ o

co [ ] e [ ] or ___

ex ___ ate

mi [ ] ___ m

br o **cc** o **l** i

i [ ] oc _____

su [ ] e [ ] f_

a [ ] a [ ] ing

a [ ] re [ ]

bi _ [ ] _ d

ne [ ] _ ___ y

di [ ] [ ] _ ar

pa [ ] a [ ] e [ ]

con [ ] en [ ] us

co [ ] i [ ] me ___

h __ mo [ ] h ___

- a vegetable
- absolutely needed
- to inject to stop disease
- vanish from sight
- weighted towards one side
- a thousand years
- achieving your aim
- a hot coffee
-
- a strong belief in or support for an idea
- remember an event
- make something much larger than it is
- serious bleeding in the body
- so bad as yo be shocking
- where you live
- agreement

202

-sion or -tion?

Easily confused? Look at the lists — then look up any words you don't know in your dictionary

mansion	admission	nation	attention
tension	inclusion	motion	condition
erosion	explosion	option	direction
evasion	excursion	caution	evolution
version	expansion	emotion	exception
mission	dimension	fiction	intention
session	collision	mention	invention
occasion	confusion	tuition	isolation
illusion	dimension	ambition	nutrition
revision	exclusion	audition	pollution
decision	conclusion	duration	accusation
omission	discussion	equation	assumption
invasion	television	location	collection
cohesion	possession	solution	congestion
division	permission	vacation	separation
adhesion	persuasion	relation	decoration

Now cover up the lists and have a go at putting in the missing 'sion' or 'tion'

op _____   man _____   ten _____   emo _____

men _____   pollu _____   audi _____   exclu _____

omis _____   occa _____   ambi _____   isola _____

persua _____   divi _____   mo _____   dimen _____

fic _____   nutri _____   televi _____   colli _____

inven _____   tui _____   confu _____   separa _____

cohe _____   dura _____   assump _____

It's On The Tip Of My Tongue!

How often has it happened to you? You almost know the word you want, but you can't quite think of it.

Use your dictionary to complete these words using the meaning and the first 3 letters given below.

next to each other	adj....................
harmless	inn....................
unwilling	rel....................
calm, peaceful	tra....................
a lack of something	def....................
present in large quantities	abu....................
upright, vertical	per....................
very small	dim....................
very, very small	min....................
lacking in self-confidence	dif....................
thick mucus in the throat	phl....................
generous, forgiving	mag....................
most typical example of its sort	epi....................
an injection	ino....................
a sad feeling	mel....................

Plus 1 Minus 1

ansered
winge
vitammin
medioccre
withold
medcine
desended
priviledge
buget
Wedesday
pattient
vicous
ficion
minusscule
phlem
courtous
farmacy
meassure
curage
circlar
viddeo
sucessful
wrectify
exaggerrate
mysterry
contemprary
vetrinary
favorite
apalling
labouratory
valuble
execise
handerchief
florescent

All the words in the list are spelled incorrectly. They have either **one** letter too many, or **one** letter too few. Write them correctly in the grid – use your dictionary if you need to.

You will reveal down the middle ladder ... a **question!**
Answer:

_ _ _ _ _ _ _ _ _ _

Can you complete these 3 words connected with the answer?

fah_ _ _ _ _ _ _ _
cen_ _ _ _ _ _ _
cel_ _ _ _

Pyramid Challenge!

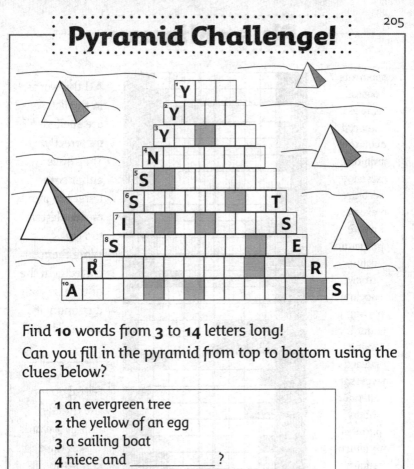

1 **Y**
2 **Y**
3 **Y**
4 **N**
5 **S**
6 **S** **T**
7 **I** **S**
8 **S** **E**
9 **R** **R**
10 **A** **S**

Find **10** words from **3** to **14** letters long!

Can you fill in the pyramid from top to bottom using the clues below?

1 an evergreen tree
2 the yellow of an egg
3 a sailing boat
4 niece and _____ ?
5 you may find one in 'bangers and mash'!
6 rank in the army or police
7 harmless
8 outline of a dark shape with light background
9 chiller cabinet in the kitchen
10 seen during breaks on TV

Jumble the shaded letters to spell one of the continents!

— — — — — — — —

Plus 1 Minus 1

separrate
posess
exsceed
cuboard
accurrate
miniture
mesenger
reconize
excert
rythm
refridgerator
colum
truely
choclate
playright
gard
ryme
suceed
neccessary
callendar
libary
parallell
arguement
sugest
Artic
garantee
hansome
Parliment
playgue
accomodate
sive
juce
dout
gilty
recipt
letuce

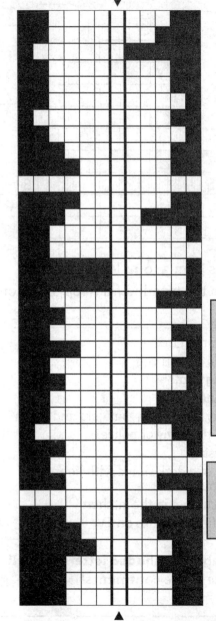

All the words in the list are spelled incorrectly. They have either **one** letter too many, or **one** letter too few. Write them correctly in the grid – use your dictionary if you need to.

You will reveal down the middle ladder **7** words which have something in common.

What is the **mnemonic** which connects them?

It's On The Tip Of My Tongue!

How often has it happened to you? You almost know the word you want, but you can't quite think of it.

Use your dictionary to complete these words using the meaning and the first 3 letters given below.

having two possible meanings	amb.................
last but one	pen.................
a type of ground pepper	pap.................
an order forbidding people to be out of their home after a certain time	cur.................
dreamlike	sur.................
state of confusion	pan.................
having a bright, hopeful outlook	opt.................
Islamic daily fasting period	Ram.................
fierce, threateningly aggressive	tru.................
any flesh-eating animal	car.................
someone who thinks that things will always turn out badly	pes.................
a 4-sided figure with just two of them parallel	tra.................
careful and accurate about small details	met.................
a yellowish-brown spice	cin.................

Plus 1 Minus 1

adress
labbel
forreigner
commitee
eigth
essppresso
amatur
untill
manoevre
suprise
cinamon
Janruary
vacum
disapeared
unskillful
irrittable
sattellite
tomorow
beleve
vegtables
definit
gage
occassion
memmento
pharoh
avertise
disasterous
amster
excelent
goverment
casles
fullfil
weired
yieled

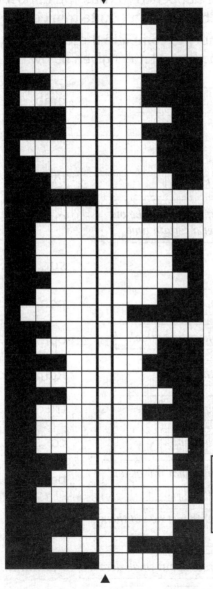

All the words in the list are spelled incorrectly. They have either **one** letter too many, or **one** letter too few. Write them correctly in the grid – use your dictionary if you need to.

You will reveal **6** words down the middle ladder. What are the missing **3**?

What is the **mnemonic** which connects them?

Pyramid Challenge!

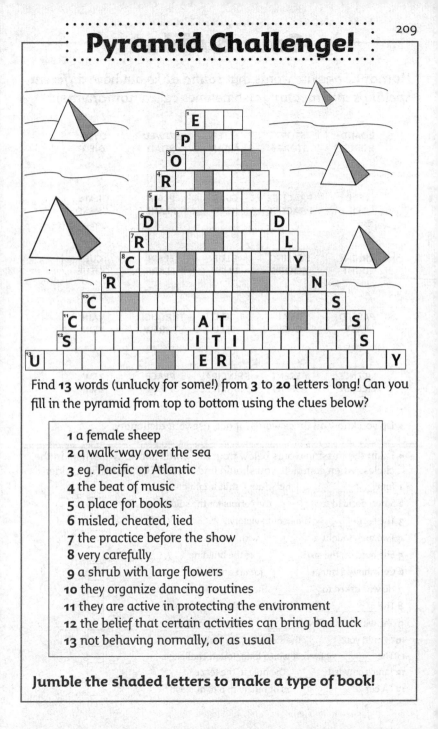

Find **13** words (unlucky for some!) from **3** to **20** letters long! Can you fill in the pyramid from top to bottom using the clues below?

1 a female sheep
2 a walk-way over the sea
3 eg. Pacific or Atlantic
4 the beat of music
5 a place for books
6 misled, cheated, lied
7 the practice before the show
8 very carefully
9 a shrub with large flowers
10 they organize dancing routines
11 they are active in protecting the environment
12 the belief that certain activities can bring bad luck
13 not behaving normally, or as usual

Jumble the shaded letters to make a type of book!

Sound Alike!

Homophones are words that *sound alike* but have *different spellings and meanings* (sometimes called **homonyms**).

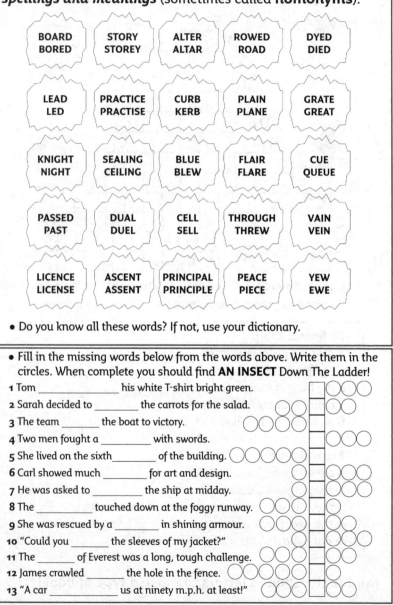

BOARD BORED	STORY STOREY	ALTER ALTAR	ROWED ROAD	DYED DIED
LEAD LED	PRACTICE PRACTISE	CURB KERB	PLAIN PLANE	GRATE GREAT
KNIGHT NIGHT	SEALING CEILING	BLUE BLEW	FLAIR FLARE	CUE QUEUE
PASSED PAST	DUAL DUEL	CELL SELL	THROUGH THREW	VAIN VEIN
LICENCE LICENSE	ASCENT ASSENT	PRINCIPAL PRINCIPLE	PEACE PIECE	YEW EWE

- Do you know all these words? If not, use your dictionary.

- Fill in the missing words below from the words above. Write them in the circles. When complete you should find **AN INSECT** Down The Ladder!

1 Tom _____ his white T-shirt bright green.

2 Sarah decided to _____ the carrots for the salad.

3 The team _____ the boat to victory.

4 Two men fought a _____ with swords.

5 She lived on the sixth_____ of the building.

6 Carl showed much _____ for art and design.

7 He was asked to _____ the ship at midday.

8 The _____ touched down at the foggy runway.

9 She was rescued by a _____ in shining armour.

10 "Could you _____ the sleeves of my jacket?"

11 The _____ of Everest was a long, tough challenge.

12 James crawled _____ the hole in the fence.

13 "A car _____ us at ninety m.p.h. at least!"

Jumble!

Can you jumble the letters to make words?
Each has a clue.

USIBCIT
_ _ _ _ _ _ _
a food

AMALL
○○○○○
a mammal

ONEMEAN
_ _ _ _ _ _ _
a flower

SSSSPPMIIII
○○○○○○○○○○○
a river

LESUORAC
○○○○○●○●
at a funfair

HTIEWG
_ _ _ _ _ _
heaviness

MOPIHPOPTAUS
○○○○○○○●○○○○
a mammal

KBOILES
○○○○○○○
a stone column

UNYAMHRHTSCEM
_ _ _ _ _ _ _ _ _ _ _ _ _
a flower

EFRIGAF
_ _ _ _ _ _ _
a mammal

AEIFCFNE
○○○○○○○○
found in cola and coffee

OUCTJNIN
_ _ _ _ _ _ _ _
where two roads meet

AFGEIERRRROT
○○○○○○○○●○○○
in a kitchen

PICALNIRP
○○○○○○○○○
head of a school

Now jumble the shaded letters to give ... **a country!**

○○○○○○○○○○○○○○○○
_ _ _ _ _ _ _ _ _ _ _ _ _ _ _ _

Sound Alike!

Homophones are words that *sound alike* but have *different spellings and meanings* (sometimes called **homonyms**).

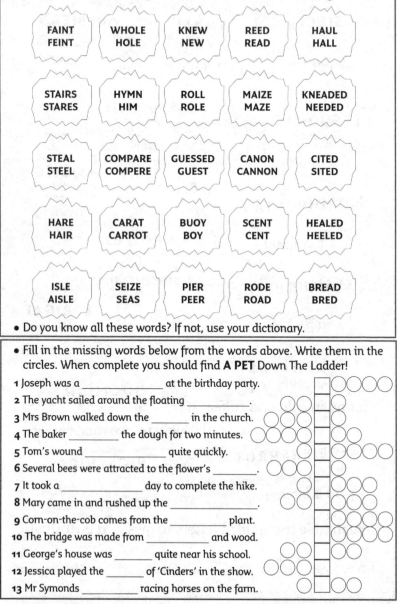

FAINT FEINT	WHOLE HOLE	KNEW NEW	REED READ	HAUL HALL
STAIRS STARES	HYMN HIM	ROLL ROLE	MAIZE MAZE	KNEADED NEEDED
STEAL STEEL	COMPARE COMPERE	GUESSED GUEST	CANON CANNON	CITED SITED
HARE HAIR	CARAT CARROT	BUOY BOY	SCENT CENT	HEALED HEELED
ISLE AISLE	SEIZE SEAS	PIER PEER	RODE ROAD	BREAD BRED

• Do you know all these words? If not, use your dictionary.

• Fill in the missing words below from the words above. Write them in the circles. When complete you should find **A PET** Down The Ladder!

1 Joseph was a _____ at the birthday party.

2 The yacht sailed around the floating _____.

3 Mrs Brown walked down the _____ in the church.

4 The baker _____ the dough for two minutes.

5 Tom's wound _____ quite quickly.

6 Several bees were attracted to the flower's _____.

7 It took a _____ day to complete the hike.

8 Mary came in and rushed up the _____.

9 Corn-on-the-cob comes from the _____ plant.

10 The bridge was made from _____ and wood.

11 George's house was _____ quite near his school.

12 Jessica played the _____ of 'Cinders' in the show.

13 Mr Symonds _____ racing horses on the farm.

Jumble!

Can you jumble the letters to make words?
Each has a clue.

FADDOFLI
_ _ _ _ _ _ _ _
a flower

UUTMAN
_ _ _ _ _ _
a season

UMUROHOS
_ _ _ _ _ _ _ _
funny

TAGUAE
_ _ _ _ _ _
a cake

OPATHISL
_ _ _ _ _ _ _ _
where the sick are treated

ESIUGSID
_ _ _ _ _ _ _ _
worn to alter appearance

INELTCAR
_ _ _ _ _ _ _ _
musical instrument

ACEUSR
_ _ _ _ _ _
under a cup!

ELWEJELYR
_ _ _ _ _ _ _ _ _
rings, necklaces, brooches

TEPANHLE
_ _ _ _ _ _ _ _
a mammal

DERNERAENATIM
_ _ _ _ _ _ _ _ _ _ _ _ _
a sea south of Europe

HEACETH
_ _ _ _ _ _ _
a very fast cat!

TSMEHCIRY
_ _ _ _ _ _ _ _ _
a science

YICPSSH
_ _ _ _ _ _ _
... and another one

NOISIVELET
_ _ _ _ _ _ _ _ _ _
TV!

Now jumble the shaded letters to give ...
a **U.S. State!**

◯ ◯ ◯ ◯ ◯ ◯ ◯ ◯ ◯ ◯

_ _ _ _ _ _ _ _ _ _

Sound Alike!

Homophones are words that *sound alike* but have *different spellings and meanings* (sometimes called **homonyms**).

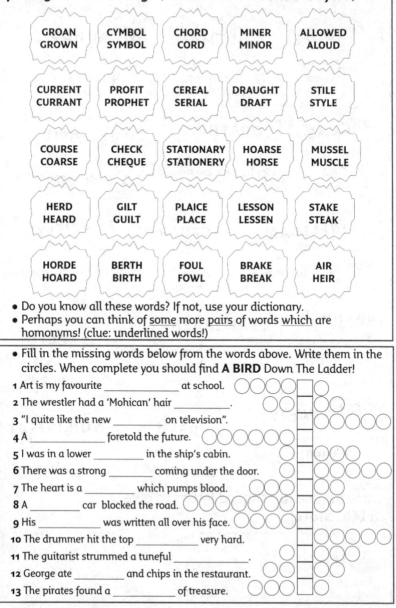

GROAN GROWN	CYMBOL SYMBOL	CHORD CORD	MINER MINOR	ALLOWED ALOUD
CURRENT CURRANT	PROFIT PROPHET	CEREAL SERIAL	DRAUGHT DRAFT	STILE STYLE
COURSE COARSE	CHECK CHEQUE	STATIONARY STATIONERY	HOARSE HORSE	MUSSEL MUSCLE
HERD HEARD	GILT GUILT	PLAICE PLACE	LESSON LESSEN	STAKE STEAK
HORDE HOARD	BERTH BIRTH	FOUL FOWL	BRAKE BREAK	AIR HEIR

- Do you know all these words? If not, use your dictionary.
- Perhaps you can think of <u>some</u> more <u>pairs</u> of words <u>which</u> are homonyms! (clue: underlined words!)

- Fill in the missing words below from the words above. Write them in the circles. When complete you should find **A BIRD** Down The Ladder!

1 Art is my favourite _____ at school.

2 The wrestler had a 'Mohican' hair _____.

3 "I quite like the new _____ on television".

4 A _____ foretold the future.

5 I was in a lower _____ in the ship's cabin.

6 There was a strong _____ coming under the door.

7 The heart is a _____ which pumps blood.

8 A _____ car blocked the road.

9 His _____ was written all over his face.

10 The drummer hit the top _____ very hard.

11 The guitarist strummed a tuneful _____.

12 George ate _____ and chips in the restaurant.

13 The pirates found a _____ of treasure.

Word For Word

WOLVES and **VOWELS** are very different! ... but they *do* have something in common. Both words contain the same letters – they are **anagrams** of one another. See if you can solve these pairs of anagrams. Use the clues and your dictionary.

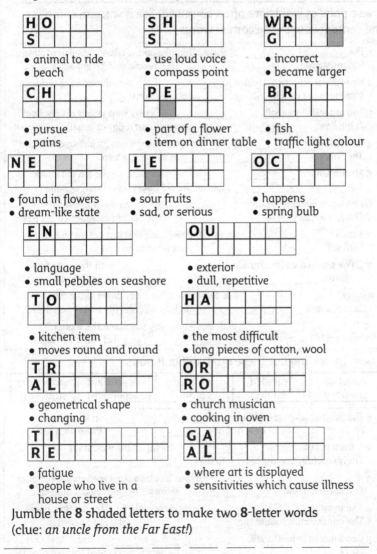

H O _ _ _
S _ _ _ _
- animal to ride
- beach

S H _ _ _
S _ _ _ _
- use loud voice
- compass point

W R _ _ _
G _ _ _ _
- incorrect
- became larger

C H _ _ _
_ _ _ _ _
- pursue
- pains

P E _ _ _
_ _ _ _ _
- part of a flower
- item on dinner table

B R _ _ _
_ _ _ _ _
- fish
- traffic light colour

N E _ _ _ _
_ _ _ _ _ _
- found in flowers
- dream-like state

L E _ _ _ _
_ _ _ _ _ _
- sour fruits
- sad, or serious

O C _ _ _ _
_ _ _ _ _ _
- happens
- spring bulb

E N _ _ _ _ _
_ _ _ _ _ _ _
- language
- small pebbles on seashore

O U _ _ _ _ _
_ _ _ _ _ _ _
- exterior
- dull, repetitive

T O _ _ _
_ _ _ _ _
- kitchen item
- moves round and round

H A _ _ _ _
_ _ _ _ _ _
- the most difficult
- long pieces of cotton, wool

T R _ _ _ _
A L _ _ _ _
- geometrical shape
- changing

O R _ _ _
R O _ _ _
- church musician
- cooking in oven

T I _ _ _ _ _
R E _ _ _ _ _
- fatigue
- people who live in a house or street

G A _ _ _ _ _
A L _ _ _ _ _
- where art is displayed
- sensitivities which cause illness

Jumble the **8** shaded letters to make two **8**-letter words (clue: *an uncle from the Far East!*)

_____ _____ _____ _____ _____ _____ _____ _____

_____ _____ _____ _____ _____ _____ _____ _____

Confusables

advice	license	affect	practise	canvas
advise	licence	effect	practice	canvass

desert	lead	proceed	conquer	miner
dessert	led	precede	concur	minor

These pairs of words are often confused. See if you can complete the sentences with the correct words.

1 The _____ of the earthquake on the island was devastating.
Sad music can _____ people in different ways.

2 Newspaper reporters decided to _____ the views of residents.
Marquees are usually made of thick, water resistant _____.

3 Tom attended football _____ every Wednesday after school.
"I have to _____ for an hour a day at least!"

4 "My favourite _____ is definitely anything including chocolate!"
The Sahara _____ is in North Africa.

5 Mr Tomkinson _____ his class on the ten mile hike.
The _____ pipes in the old house were badly corroded.

6 Mrs Jones handed her driving _____ to the traffic policeman.
The farmer decided to _____ the use of pesticides on his fields.

7 Sam's _____ was to stop worrying and just get on with it.
Sam will _____ you what to do next.

8 Chloe plucked up the courage to _____ with the tricky task.
"I always _____ Christmas dinner with a brisk walk!"

9 Every _____ has to shower after a day down in the coal pit.
He received a _____ ticking off from the teacher on duty.

10 "I _____ with everything you say about the matter!"
Joe decided to try and _____ his fear of spiders.

Now try sorting out these more difficult pairs.

envelop	alluded	council	dependent	stationary
envelope	eluded	counsel	dependant	stationery

1 The flood-stricken family was _____ on help arriving.
Mr Smith said that he only had one _____ living with him.

2 A thick mist began to _____ the top of the mountain.
Emily carefully slid the letter into the _____.

3 A _____ car was blocking the supermarket entrance.
She needed a few _____ items for her homework project.

4 The town _____ are responsible for cleaning the streets.
The crime victim sought the _____ of a good solicitor.

5 Good marks in maths still _____ James and Carl.
Mr Lewis _____ that he was disappointed by their results.

Word Burgers

Choose the correct filling for each burger – to make **9-letter** words. Put each word in the answer box to reveal the vertical mystery word: *you use it at school*

BURGER FILLINGS	
ALL	PEN
END	CAN
ICE	LOW
NIT	DEN
LET	ERA

1 ATH _ _ _ ICS

2 GEN _ _ _ LLY

3 MED _ _ _ IST

4 MAD _ _ _ ING

5 CAR _ _ _ TER

6 LEG _ _ _ ARY

7 FUR _ _ _ URE

8 BUC _ _ _ EER

9 POL _ _ _ MAN

10 BEL _ _ _ ING

Follow That Car!

See if you can work out all **10** words – they all have 'CAR' in them

car _ _ _ _   a mobile holiday home

car _ _ _ _   a chewy sweet

car _ _ _ _ _   a woollen jacket

_ car _ _ _   a red colour

car _   a stiff paper

car _ _ _ _ _ _   looks after a school

car _ _ _ _ _ _ _   a garden flower

_ car _   a winter neck warmer

car _ _ _ _   cautious

_ car _ _ _ _ _   frightens birds

At-TEN-tion!

See if you can work out all **12** words – they all have 'TEN' in them

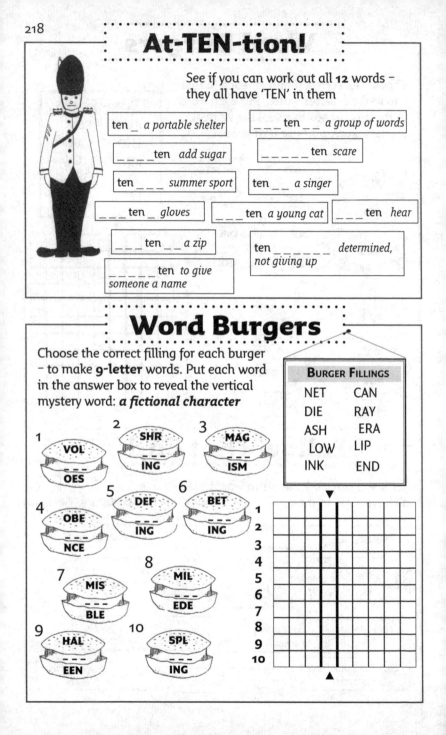

ten _   *a portable shelter*

_ _ _ _ ten _ _   *a group of words*

_ _ _ _ ten   *add sugar*

_ _ _ _ _ _ ten   *scare*

ten _ _ _   *summer sport*

ten _ _   *a singer*

_ _ _ ten _   *gloves*

_ _ _ ten   *a young cat*

_ _ _ ten   *hear*

_ _ _ ten _ _   *a zip*

ten _ _ _ _ _ _   *determined, not giving up*

_ _ _ _ _ _ ten   *to give someone a name*

Word Burgers

Choose the correct filling for each burger – to make **9-letter** words. Put each word in the answer box to reveal the vertical mystery word: *a fictional character*

BURGER FILLINGS

NET	CAN
DIE	RAY
ASH	ERA
LOW	LIP
INK	END

1. VOL _ _ _ OES
2. SHR _ _ _ ING
3. MAG _ _ _ ISM
4. OBE _ _ _ NCE
5. DEF _ _ _ ING
6. BET _ _ _ ING
7. MIS _ _ _ BLE
8. MIL _ _ _ EDE
9. HAL _ _ _ EEN
10. SPL _ _ _ ING

1
2
3
4
5
6
7
8
9
10

Word Burgers

Choose the correct filling for each burger – to make **9-letter** words. Put each word in the answer box to reveal the vertical mystery word.

BURGER FILLINGS	
ONE	RAT
CAT	SAG
OUT	ROW
DEN	SON
ARM	SIT

1. EDU _ _ _ ION
2. NAR _ _ _ EST
3. OPP _ _ _ NTS
4. SEN _ _ _ IVE
5. PRI _ _ _ ERS
6. OPE _ _ _ ION
7. SPR _ _ _ ING
8. SPE _ _ _ INT
9. GAR _ _ _ ING
10. NEW _ _ _ ENT

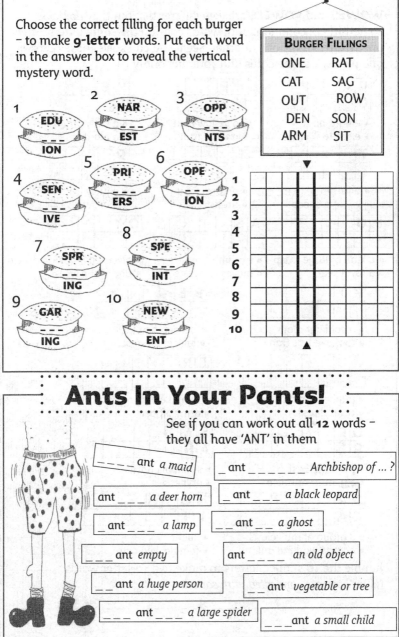

Ants In Your Pants!

See if you can work out all **12** words – they all have 'ANT' in them

_ _ _ _ ant *a maid*	_ ant _ _ _ _ _ _ *Archbishop of … ?*
ant _ _ _ *a deer horn*	_ ant _ _ _ *a black leopard*
_ ant _ _ _ *a lamp*	_ _ ant _ _ *a ghost*
_ _ _ ant *empty*	ant _ _ _ _ *an old object*
_ _ ant *a huge person*	_ _ ant *vegetable or tree*
_ _ _ _ ant _ _ _ *a large spider*	_ _ _ ant *a small child*

Word For Word

WOLVES and **VOWELS** are very different! ... but they *do* have something in common. Both words contain the same letters – they are **anagrams** of one another. See if you can solve these pairs of anagrams. Use the clues and your dictionary.

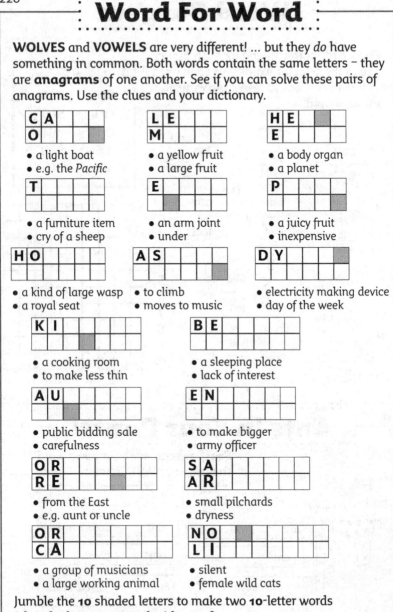

C A _ _ _ _
O _ _ _ ▨
- a light boat
- e.g. the *Pacific*

L E _ _ _
M _ _ _ _
- a yellow fruit
- a large fruit

H E _ ▨ _
E _ _ _ _
- a body organ
- a planet

T _ _ _
_ _ _ _
- a furniture item
- cry of a sheep

E _ ▨ _ _
_ _ _ _ _
- an arm joint
- under

P _ _ _ ▨
_ _ _ _ _
- a juicy fruit
- inexpensive

H O _ _ _ _
_ _ _ _ _ _
- a kind of large wasp
- a royal seat

A S _ _ _ ▨
_ _ _ _ _ _
- to climb
- moves to music

D Y _ _ _ ▨
_ _ _ _ _ _
- electricity making device
- day of the week

K I _ ▨ _ _
_ _ _ _ _ _
- a cooking room
- to make less thin

B E _ _ _ _
_ _ _ _ _ _
- a sleeping place
- lack of interest

A U _ _ _ _
_ ▨ _ _ _ _
- public bidding sale
- carefulness

E N _ _ _ _
_ _ _ _ _ _
- to make bigger
- army officer

O R _ _ _ _
R E _ _ _ ▨ _
- from the East
- e.g. aunt or uncle

S A _ _ _ _
A R _ _ _ _
- small pilchards
- dryness

O R _ _ _ _ _
C A _ _ _ _ _
- a group of musicians
- a large working animal

N O _ ▨ _ _ _
L I _ _ _ _ _
- silent
- female wild cats

Jumble the **10** shaded letters to make two **10**-letter words
(clue: *both are connected with sound*)

_ _ _ _ _   _ _ _ _ _

_ _ _ _ _   _ _ _ _ _

Confusables

premiere premier	imminent eminent	excerpt exert	among amid

serial cereal	device devise	hangar hanger	accept except	excess access

These pairs of words are often confused. See if you can complete the sentences with the correct words.

1 Sarah put her new jacket on the _____ behind the door.
   The jet fighters were in a line in the large aircraft _____.

2 There was an _____ of smoke pouring from the chimney.
   _____ to the building was restricted by all the parked cars.

3 He was, without doubt, the _____ footballer of his generation.
   The evening _____ of the musical was a very lavish occasion.

4 The audience cheered wildly at the _____ arrival of the pop star.
   The most _____ person at the fair was the mayor.

5 They saw an _____ from the movie on television during the weekend.
   Darren had to _____ himself to haul in the heavy fishing net.

6 The children ate their picnic lunches _____ a sea of bluebells.
   Julie stood _____ the small crowd outside the shop.

7 The clever _____ helped the disabled lady to turn on the tap.
   "I shall _____ a plan to beat him at his own game," said James.

8 The television _____ had all the viewers glued to their seats.
   For breakfast Joanne chose _____ , toast, and coffee.

9 "Please _____ this gift on behalf of all the pupils," said the headmaster.
   They all came to the party _____ Jane and Jonathon.

alternative alternate	continuous continual	complement compliment	principal principle

Now try sorting out these more difficult pairs.

1 The country bus service only ran on _____ weekdays starting Mondays.
   Considering her position she had no _____ but to agree.

2 The college _____ was the chairman of the committee.
   "Caring for others" is the first _____ of our school.

3 There were _____ outbreaks of talking which ruined the show.
   The _____ roar of the swollen river prevented her from sleeping all night.

4 "My finished painting earned me a _____ from my dad for a change!"
   "We now have a full _____ of pupils ready to start the exam."

Sssh! Quiet Please!

Can you fill in all the silent letters?

1 _ rong

2 _ nuckle

3 dou _ t

4 _ rapper

5 colum _

6 _ reath

7 s _ ience

8 _ onesty

9 _ naw

10 lam _

11 lis _ en

12 _ hole

13 _ nock

14 this _ le

15 _ nat

16 crum _ s

17 rus _ le

18 w _ ich

19 _ narled

20 solem _

21 plum _ er

22 mus _ le

23 _ nu

24 _ cimitar

25 jos _ le

Word Search

Now see if you can find all but one of the 25 'silent letter' words in the grid – they are in all directions except diagonally. Which is the missing word?

```
P H C I H W G N A W E O Q R W S
L D O U B T Z Y N E L T S U R C
U N M U L O C P C B T P A O E I
M J L X E F E D M U S C L E A M
B X W R A P P E R Q O R N L T I
E D E L R A N G R K J U M T H T
R I L A W U T J S D J M R S Q A
E W K M V W R O N G U B S I U R
L X C B E Y X U L W M S R H T G
O Y U N G Z K C O N K C V T S N
H H N M E L O S B N E T S I L A
W G K F D A V T Y T S E N O H T
```

Heads and Tails

Grid	Clue
P _ _ R • • • • •	a fruit
P _ _ R • • • • •	a couple
P _ _ L • • • • •	skin of fruit
P _ _ L • • • • •	sound of bells
C _ _ R • • • •	group of singers
A _ _ E • • • •	quick, nimble
I _ _ E • • • •	angry
P _ _ E • • • •	part of a larger object
F _ _ E • • •	decorative border
O _ _ E • • •	not transparent
E _ _ D • • •	heard again
A _ _ R • • •	it moors a ship
A _ _ S • •	worried
A _ _ R • •	not professional
V _ _ E • •	car, tractor, bus
F _ _ E • •	easily broken
R _ _ S •	very hungry
R _ _ E •	trustworthy
A _ _ E •	spot on, precise
L _ _ E •	e.g. French, Spanish
N _ _ Y	needed
R _ _ E	identify, know
P _ _ L	continual, eternal
P _ _ T	fixed, unchanged
N _ _ L	active by night
C _ _ S	awake, not asleep
H _ _ S	very funny

1. Fill in the 27 words to match the clues. We have given you their first and last letters.

2. Jumble the letters in the shaded squares to make a 9-letter word. *Clue*: an occupation

3. Complete the crossword grid opposite with the same 27 words.

Heads and Tails

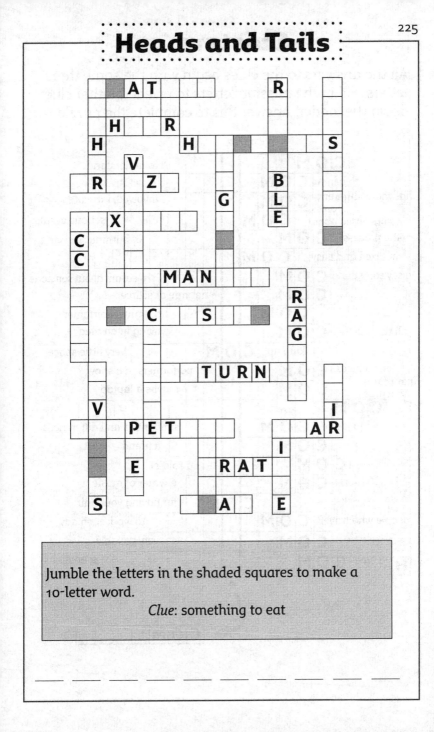

Jumble the letters in the shaded squares to make a 10-letter word.

Clue: something to eat

Starters...

All the answers to the clues begin with the same three letters. Fill in the missing letters to reveal another clue down the ladder. Answer this to complete the puzzle.

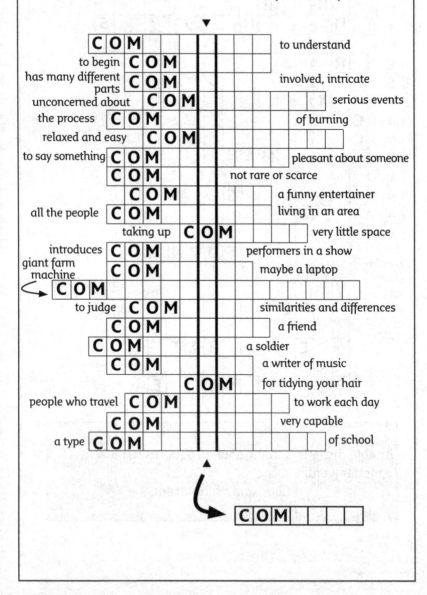

Clue (left)	Answer	Clue (right)
	C O M	to understand
to begin	**C O M**	
has many different parts	**C O M**	involved, intricate
unconcerned about	**C O M**	serious events
the process	**C O M**	of burning
relaxed and easy	**C O M**	
to say something	**C O M**	pleasant about someone
	C O M	not rare or scarce
	C O M	a funny entertainer
all the people	**C O M**	living in an area
taking up	**C O M**	very little space
introduces	**C O M**	performers in a show
giant farm machine	**C O M**	maybe a laptop
	C O M	
to judge	**C O M**	similarities and differences
	C O M	a friend
	C O M	a soldier
	C O M	a writer of music
	C O M	for tidying your hair
people who travel	**C O M**	to work each day
	C O M	very capable
a type	**C O M**	of school

C O M _ _ _

Word Search

C	A	R	R	O	T	C	A	R	R	Y	C	J
A	C	L	C	A	R	C	A	S	S	O	A	C
R	A	C	A	R	A	F	E	M	C	S	R	A
A	R	S	S	C	A	R	E	T	A	K	E	R
M	G	X	C	A	R	P	E	T	R	C	F	P
E	O	C	A	R	E	E	R	C	N	A	R	M
L	C	A	T	B	R	F	C	A	A	R	E	Y
C	A	R	T	O	O	N	A	R	T	A	E	C
A	R	E	J	N	C	Q	R	P	I	V	Z	A
R	N	F	C	N	A	C	D	E	O	A	C	R
D	A	U	A	C	R	A	I	N	N	N	A	R
I	G	L	R	A	T	R	G	T	Q	X	R	I
N	E	F	V	R	O	A	A	E	Y	J	T	O
A	G	H	E	E	N	T	B	R	L	O	T	N
L	C	A	R	D	I	A	C	C	A	R	O	L

1. _____
2. _____
3. _____
4. _____
5. _____
6. _____
7. _____
8. _____
9. _____
10. _____
11. _____
12. _____
13. _____
14. _____
15. _____
16. _____
17. _____
18. _____
19. _____
20. _____
21. _____
22. _____
23. _____
24. _____
25. _____
26. _____
27. _____
28. _____

Can you find all 28 words in the grid using the clues below? All of them begin with 'CAR' so use your dictionary to help. In the grid the words are all written across or down, not backwards or diagonally. We've started you off with one – 'CARPET'

1. a sweet
2. comic drawing
3. e.g. charcoal
4. looks after school
5. high ranking priest
6. vegetable
7. life work, occupation
8. a ship's load
9. body of a dead animal
10. cautious

11. garden flower
12. ~~floor covering~~
13. wood worker
14. woollen jacket
15. relating to the heart
16. gold purity measure
17. towed by car
18. wine serving bottle
19. having no worries
20. slaughter, killing

21. freshwater fish
22. rotting animal flesh
23. pick up and take
24. cardboard container
25. shape by cutting
26. Christmas hymn
27. horse drawn vehicle
28. protection, keeping

HAPPY SEARCHING!

Starters...

All the answers to the clues begin with the same three letters. Fill in the missing letters to reveal another clue down the ladder. Answer this to complete the puzzle.

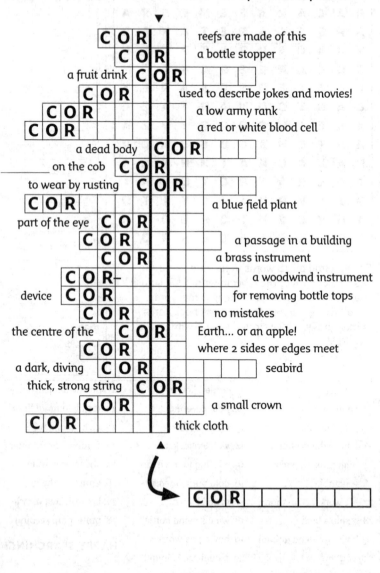

C O R		reefs are made of this
C O R		a bottle stopper
a fruit drink **C O R**		
C O R		used to describe jokes and movies!
C O R		a low army rank
C O R		a red or white blood cell
a dead body **C O R**		
_____ on the cob **C O R**		
to wear by rusting **C O R**		
C O R		a blue field plant
part of the eye **C O R**		
C O R		a passage in a building
C O R		a brass instrument
C O R		a woodwind instrument
device **C O R**		for removing bottle tops
C O R		no mistakes
the centre of the **C O R**		Earth... or an apple!
C O R		where 2 sides or edges meet
a dark, diving **C O R**		seabird
thick, strong string **C O R**		
C O R		a small crown
C O R		thick cloth

C O R ▢ ▢ ▢ ▢ ▢ ▢

Jumble!

This time can you jumble the words to make a single word ... there is a link between the given words and the solutions!

e.g. NO STAMP = POSTMAN!

There are some illustrations to help you.

FIR CONE
_ _ _ _ _ _ _

MOUTH CASE
_ _ _ _ _ _ _ _ _

SEA TRIP
_ _ _ _ _ _ _

A STEW SIR?
_ _ _ _ _ _ _ _

GO NURSE
_ _ _ _ _ _ _

LITHE ACTS
_ _ _ _ _ _ _ _ _

FLUTTER BY
_ _ _ _ _ _ _ _ _

MOON STARER
_ _ _ _ _ _ _ _ _ _

IT EGGS US ON
_ _ _ _ _ _ _ _ _

SLID THERE
_ _ _ _ _ _ _ _ _

HINT! HINT!

UNTO A STAR
_ _ _ _ _ _ _ _ _

October 24th
October 31st

STOPPED? NO!
_ _ _ _ _ _ _ _ _

BEAR HIT DEN!
_ _ _ _ _ _ _ _ _

MINUS LACE
_ _ _ _ _ _ _ _

TAKE MR PURSE
_ _ _ _ _ _ _ _ _ _

Heads and Tails

M			H	•	•	•	•	•	untrue story, legend
D			T	•	•	•	•	•	sum of money covered
O			T	•	•	•	•	•	leave out
H			X	•	•	•	•	•	trick, deception
Q			E	•	•	•	•	•	a line of people
B			E	•	•	•	•	•	pale creamy brown
D			T	•	•	•	•	•	a person's first performance
V			L	•	•	•	•	•	a strong plastic
R				M	•	•	•	•	musical beat
B				D	•	•	•	•	favoured unfairly
A				T	•	•	•	•	not present at school
I				L	•	•	•	•	a Middle-Eastern nation
B					T	•	•	•	obvious
H					E	•	•	•	cleanliness
D					E	•	•	•	to mislead
A					D	•	•	•	opposite of departed
C						R	•	•	shows months and days
P						L	•	•	on time
D						R	•	•	width of a circle
A						T	•	•	a quarrel
C							R	•	someone standing for election
I							S	•	a type of triangle
V							R	•	someone who does unpaid work
B							L	•	attractive, pleasing
P							R	•	a university teacher
S							N	•	king or queen
I							Y	•	a plan of a journey

1. Fill in the 27 words to match the clues. We have given you their first and last letters.

2. Jumble the letters in the shaded squares to make a 9-letter word. *Clue*: a creature with a very special talent!

3. Complete the crossword grid opposite with the same 27 words.

Heads and Tails

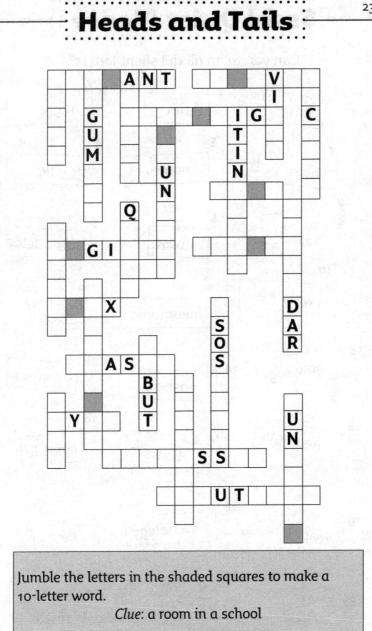

Jumble the letters in the shaded squares to make a 10-letter word.

Clue: a room in a school

Sssh! Quiet Please !

Can you fill in all the silent letters?

1 clim _

2 thum _

3 _ night

4 hym _

5 _ nome

6 su _ tle

7 ca _ m

8 _ onest

9 mis _ letoe

10 whis _ le

11 _ neumonia

12 _ rong

13 _ nowledge

14 _ nashed

15 r _ ythm

16 _ neumatic

17 s _ issors

18 cas _ le

19 _ reck

20 _ sychology

21 de _ t

22 _ rist

23 g _ ost

24 _ rinkle

25 recei _ t

ANSWERS TO EXERCISES

Exercise 1

1. lis**t**en, mus**c**le, has**t**en, com**b**, autum**n**, glis**t**en, hym**n**, dou**b**t, colum**n**, s**c**ience, solem**n**, lim**b**, this**t**le, s**c**issors, fas**t**en, de**b**t, cas**t**le, dou**b**t, s**c**ene, condem**n**

2.

silent w	silent k	silent g
writer	knowledge	gnat
wrestle	knock	sign
wrench	kneel	gnarl
wrist	knight	
wry	knuckle	
Wrong		

3. **p**neumonia, **p**terodactyl, **p**salm, **p**sychology

4. **Christian** walked down the street. It was an **autumn** day and the colourful trees **glistened** in the morning light.
"What a wonderful **scene**," he said to himself.

He was a **scientist** who studied **psychology** as a
student. He was looking for a road **sign** to find his tutor.
He had **written** an essay showing off his **knowledge**
and he was keen to show his tutor. He **hastened** his
step. He mustn't take the **wrong** road. He gave a **wry**
smile to himself; he **knew** he would get A+ for this work
– no **doubt** at all.

5. peace *piece*   ceiling **sealing**   board **bored**
   break **brake**

   vain **vein**   duel **dual**   led **lead**
   flair **flare**   whole **hole**

   steak **stake**   sent **scent**   right **write/rite**
   altar **alter**   coarse **course**

6. John was busy preparing to open his music shop in the
   High Street. He had already received his **licence** from
   the record companies who, in **principle**, are happy for
   small shops to sell their products. The biggest hurdle
   to clear was to work out a **draft** agreement with the
   local **councillor**. It took time for him to **accept** all **their**
   terms of trading, but John took plenty of **advice** and
   made sure he got his **story** straight. All the paperwork
   seemed to take **too** long, but eventually the deal was
   signed. John had always wanted to have his own shop

because he had a *flair* for business. Next, he got all the *stationery* and promotional materials printed and he was ready to open his doors. He was keeping his fingers crossed that the opening day would see a *horde* of people in a *queue* outside.

Exercise 2

1. The young prince's r**ei**gn as King began when he bec**a**me **eigh**teen. He promised to honour and ob**ey** and to conv**ey** the right w**ay** for the country to beh**ave**

2. The l**ea**der of the local council agr**ee**d that the committ**ee** should have a good r**ea**son to delay its next m**ee**ting. It should not dec**ei**ve the public or imp**ede** the work of the attorn**ey** who was costing a lot of mon**ey**.

3. The p**y**thon was so powerful it paral**y**sed its prey. The zoo keeper had to ident**i**f**y** the wildl**i**fe that d**i**ed and f**i**le a report. None of the animals could be rev**i**ved.

4. The g**o**at was al**o**ne in the mead**ow**. It ch**o**ked on a piece of t**o**ast it had ch**o**sen to swall**ow**.

5. The stat**ue** was **u**seless and had no val**ue**. It was moved to a n**ew** ven**ue** to subd**ue** those who took the vi**ew** that the **U**nited Nations didn't have a cl**ue** about art.

6. horses, gateaux, curries, knives, families, videos, matches

7. The old *ladies* looked at *their photos*. *They* showed *their families* when they were young.
They brought back *some* happy *memories*. *They* had enjoyed *their parties* and seemed not to have *any worries*. How their lives had changed. The *stories they* would tell *their* grandchildren!

8. mice, sheep, fungi/funguses, oxen, dice, lice

9. roves, vallies, echos, cowes, leafs, skys, potatos, tomatos, greenhouse's, worrys, chicken's, wolfs, bushs, field's, lorrys, wolfs, themselves, loafs, animal's, chicken's

Exercise 3

1. ART: display, highlight, spectrum

DT: tension

ENGLISH: prefix, suffix

GEOG: atlas, climate, landscape

HIST: conflict

IT: hardware, password

MATHS: reflect

SCIENCE: absorb, exchange, insect

2.

Art	perspective dimension
DT	component specification presentation
English	consonant metaphor alliteration exclamation personification vocabulary
Geography	habitat longitude infrastructure international

History	government parliament propaganda Protestant
IT	electronic interactive
Maths	denominator negative circumference equilateral multiplication quadrilateral
Science	predator apparatus laboratory temperature

3. child   *children, childish, childless, childhood, childlike*

   take   *mistaken, mistake, overtaken, overtaking, partaking*

   public *publicity, publication*

   bore   *boredom, boring*

   pass   *passenger, passage*

   sign   *signatory, signature, signal, resign, resignation*

cover	*discover, discovery*
medic	*medical, medication*
electric	*electrician, electricity, electronic, electrical, electrocute*
give	*given, forgiveness*

Exercise 4

1.

inaccurate	immature	irregular	illegal
incapable	improper	irresponsible	illegible
indecent	impolite	irresistible	illiterate

misplace	nonsmoker	unhelpful	antibiotic
misread	nonstop	unlikely	anticlockwise
misfire	nonstick	unrealistic	anticlimax

2.

in	*not or the opposite of*
im	*not or the opposite of*
ir	*not or the opposite of*
il	*not or the opposite of*
mis	*wrong or false*
non	*not*
un	*opposite of*
anti	*opposed or opposite to*

3. (a) Turn the handle **anti**clockwise.

(b) I am quite **in**capable of doing that!

(c) I have **mis**placed my glasses somewhere.

(d) That girl is very **im**mature.

(e) Is it **il**legal to park here?

4. The following are only suggestions. 'Mad', for example, can form 'madness' and 'madly'.

hope**less**
child**like**
enjoy**ment**
mad**ness**
friend**ship**
king**dom**
sudden**ly**
wonder**ful**

5. The following sentences are just examples. Ask a teacher or parent to check yours.

They live in my neighbour**hood**.
They have a good friend**ship**.
Eating straight before going swimming is mad**ness**.
He was hope**less** at playing football.
He was sick of her child**like** behaviour.

6. (a) He carry + *ed* the shopping all the way to his flat.
(Rule: *change y*)

(b) We were chuckle + *ing* about the joke on the TV.
(Rule: *drop e*)

(c) Alice was dream + *ing* about the holiday she would
have. (Rule: *add*)

(d) Wayne has been drop + *ed* from the football team.
(Rule: *double*)

(e) He was hope + *ing* to get a Saturday job in the High
Street. (Rule: *drop e*)

(f) Dad was strip + *ing* the wallpaper from the kitchen
wall. (Rule: *double*)

(g) "I'm not doing that!" I reply + *ed* quickly. (Rule:
change y)

(h) The frost disappear + *ed* from the grass as soon as
the sun came out. (Rule: *add*)

(i) The evidence was bury + *ed* in the ground.
(Rule: *change y*)

7.

	Prefix	Base word	Suffix
irreplaceable	ir-	replace	-able
irremovable	ir-	remove	-able
insincerely	in-	sincere	-ly
uncomfortable	un-	comfort	-able
impossibility	im-	possible	-ity

unhappiness	un-	happy	-ness
antiheroes	anti-	hero	-es
miscommunication	mis-	communicate	-tion

Exercise 5

1. Astronaut, biography, century, duodenum, photograph, octagon, claustrophobia, photocopy, microscope, visible

2. **aero** means involving the air, the atmosphere, or aircraft

   aerodynamic having a streamlined shape that moves easily through the air

   aeroplane a vehicle with wings and engines that enable it to fly

   aqua means 'water'

   aquarium a glass tank filled with water in which fish are kept

   aquatic involving water

   aqueduct a long bridge with many arches carrying a water supply over a valley

   audi means involving hearing or sound

audible loud enough to be heard

audience a group of people listening (and sometimes watching) a performance

audition a short performance given by a musician or actor, so their skills can be assessed for a position in an orchestra or part in a play or film

geo means 'earth'

geology the study of the earth's structure, especially the layers of rock and soil that make up the surface of the earth

geography the study of the physical features of the earth, together with the climate, natural resources and population in different parts of the world

geometry the branch of mathematics that deals with lines, angles, curves, and spaces

ped means foot or feet

pedal a control lever on a machine or vehicle that you press with your foot

pedestrian someone who is walking

quadruped any animal with four legs

scope means an instrument used for observing or detecting

microscope a piece of equipment that magnifies very small objects so that you can study them

telescope a long instrument shaped like a tube, which has lenses that make distant objects appear larger and nearer

stethoscope a device used by doctors to listen to a patient's heart and breathing

tri means three

triangle a shape with three straight sides

triathlon a sports contest in which athlete compete in three different events

trilogy a series of three books or plays that have the same characters or are on the same subject

ANSWERS TO PUZZLES

One Too Many

tomorrow, rhinoceros, separate, sandwich, disappeared,
query, sugar, luxurious, inoculate, necessary
GYMNASTICS

1 Missing

(I) (H) (A) (O) (L) (Y) (D) = HOLIDAY

(M) (R) (R) (O) (E) (I) (D) (R) = MIRRORED

Tricky Eights!

separate, accident, commence, definite, nuisance,
humorous, spacious, brochure, boutique, sandwich,
electric, thorough

Tricky Sevens!

excited, leisure, jealous, exclaim, snorkel, despair, exceeds,
anoraks, centres, foreign, century, excerpt

One In Four

temperature, parallel, millionaire, rhythm, jealousy,
hygiene, pigeon, xylophone
SANDWICH

At The Zoo

The *journey* to the zoo last *Wednesday* was a *great success*, *except* for me having an *argument* with my best *friend*. You'll never *believe* what about! The *fillings* in our *sandwiches*! Still, when we got *there* we were best mates *again*!

It's a good job *too*, otherwise we wouldn't have enjoyed the animals. We saw some *beautiful giraffes* and *their neighbours*, the *fascinating gorillas* with *their enormous muscles*. My *favourites* were the artic *foxes*, the *spotted leopards* and the *miniature horses*.

We had dinner in a *lovely restaurant although* the *vegetables* were a bit under cooked *especially* the *potatoes*! However, the *vanilla ice-cream* was *delicious*. During the afternoon I was *disappointed because* the *temperature* dropped and *there* was an *autumn* storm. *Lightning* flashed and it *really poured* down so we *sheltered*. The rain soon stopped *though*, but it was *nearly* as cold as *February*!

Still, it was an *excellent* day, *which* I will never forget, *except* for the *stomach ache* I had *through* eating one of my best *friend's sandwiches*!

1 Missing

achieve, broccoli, anaesthetic, vehicle, environment, fascinated, disappointed   SPINACH
gorgeous, analysis, margarine, miniature, Caribbean, camouflage, embarrass, coffee   FEBRUARY

One In Four

①(A)(M)(D)(Y)(P)(S)(R) = **PYRAMIDS**

Tricky Eights

definite, occasion, business, excerpts, aqueduct, schedule, mimicked, mortgage, grateful, equipped, surprise, guardian

Endings -er/-or/-ar

actor, popular, dollar, badger, chapter, sailor, collar, doctor, danger, father, junior, caterpillar, mirror, regular, visitor, vinegar, mother, teacher

Tricky Nines!

permanent, hypocrisy, guarantee, jewellery, facetious, advertise, itinerary, disappear, minuscule, manoeuvre, necessary, consensus

Endings -a/-our/-re

aroma, arena, orchestra, quota, sultana, panda, glamour, honour, labour, humour, vapour, favour, meagre, acre, metre, sabre, mitre, lustre

Endings -a/-our/-re

banana, rumour, neighbour, colour, litre, millimetre, centre, camera, larva, fibre, armour, kilometre, flavour, centimetre, harbour, zebra, idea, vanilla

One Too Many

(D)(R)(U)(N)(E)(I) = **RUINED**

Endings -or/-ar/-er

horror, pillar, waiter, ruler, jaguar, youngster, cedar, anchor, nectar, guitar, baker, polar, adder, equator, warrior, razor, daughter, factor

Tricky Sevens!

believe, hexagon, anxious, medical, receive, eagerly, achieve, ghastly, married, stomach, receipt, liaison

-ant or -ent?

absent, vacant, buoyant, accident, militant, parent, lenient, radiant, fragrant, permanent, adjacent, rodent, efficient, indignant, poignant, tenant, salient, hesitant, argument, coherent, tolerant, ancient, valiant, apparent, ailment

-able or -ible?

capable, gullible, legible, desirable, amiable, probable, incapable, divisible, plausible, incredible, reusable, terrible, tangible, advisable, flammable, eligible, visible, adorable, culpable, sensible, inaudible, pliable, possible, irritable, risible, durable, indelible, debatable

Down Town

It was a *miserable Saturday* morning in *January*.
Because I was a bit *bored I decided I fancied* a walk into
town. I set *off* about ten *O'clock* and *firstly headed down
our avenue*. I *passed* the *local library*, *our school* and
then *wandered through* the *deserted* park towards the
town *centre*.
It began to *drizzle* and then it *properly* pored down! I got
really soaked! *Luckily* it *stopped* after about a *quarter* of
an *hour*. At *exactly* midday I passed the fire-*station* and
to my *great surprise*, a fire-*engine* shot out and *nearly
flattened* me!
It must *have been* doing *eighty* miles-an-*hour*! At *least*!
After I *recovered* and *caught* my *breath*, *I quickly made*
for the *gigantic shopping centre*. I felt a bit peckish so *I*
had a *snack* and a *coffee* in a *little café* next door to my
favourite music store.
Then *I* met one of my mates, *Michael*.
I was *shocked* to *hear* his *news*!
He *told* me all about *his* cat being *stuck* up *their
sycamore* tree, just *down our avenue*!
"Ah! *That's where* the fire-*engine* was *speeding to*!" *I
reckoned*.
Anyway, to cut a long *story* short, *Michael invited* me to
his place, and we spent the *rest* of the *afternoon* playing
computer games in *his* room, with his *rescued ginger* cat
for *company*.
I must say that it *looked* a *touch shaken* and *nervous*!
Mind you, you'd be a bit *jumpy having been stuck* up a
tree all morning! *Wouldn't* you?

Quiz Quest!

turquoise, squirrel, oblique, mosquito, frequently, bouquet, boutique, adequate, squander, unique, bouquet, eloquent, squeamish, antique, opaque, equestrian, ubiquitous, picturesque

Starters

catapult, cathedral, category, catalogue, catastrophe, cataract, catarrh, Catholic, catflap, catamaran, catching, Catherine, catkin, catseye, caterer, catacomb, cattle
CATERPILLAR

Ladder Spell!

visitor, disappoint, suggest, allowed, building, column, designer, knee, safety, healthy, sincerely, author, giraffe, memory, attempt, architect, thermometer, conceal
SPELL LIKE A CHAMPION

One In Four

Ⓞ Ⓛ Ⓔ Ⓔ Ⓥ Ⓟ Ⓝ Ⓔ = **ENVELOPE**

Phantastic Phantoms

autograph, elephant, geography, megaphone, microphone, nephew, phantom, pharmacy, pheasant, photograph, saxophone, sphinx, paragraph, cenotaph

Ladder Spell!

surprise, relief, ancient, vinegar, salmon, receipt, suppose, jealous, friendly, fatally, ghastly, conceit, burglar, seize, parallel, visitor, knives, exercise
PINEAPPLE/TANGERINE

1 Missing

(E)(O)(S)(N)(M)(N)(W) = SNOWMEN

(N)(I)(P)(C)(A)(C)(P)(U)(O)(C) = CAPPUCCINO

Singles or Doubles?

espresso, commemorate, exaggerate, millennium, broccoli, inoculate, successful, appalling, address, biased, necessary, disappear, parallel, consensus, commitment, haemorrhage

-sion or -tion?

option, mansion, tension, emotion, mention, pollution, audition, exclusion, omission, occasion, ambition, isolation, persuasion, division, motion, dimension, fiction, nutrition, television, collision, invention, tuition, confusion, separation, cohesion, duration, assumption

It's On The Tip Of My Tongue!

adjacent, innocuous, reluctant, tranquil, deficiency, abundant, perpendicular, diminutive, minuscule, diffident, phlegm, magnanimous, epitome, inoculation, melancholy

Plus 1 Minus 1

answered, whinge, vitamin, mediocre, withhold, medicine, descended, privilege, budget, Wednesday, patient, vicious, fiction, minuscule, phlegm, courteous, pharmacy, measure, courage, circular, video, successful, rectify, exaggerate, mystery, contemporary, veterinary, favourite, appalling, laboratory, valuable, exercise, handkerchief, fluorescent

which invention measures temperatures? = **THERMOMETER**

Pyramid Challenge

yew, yolk, yacht, nephew, sausage, sergeant, innocuous, silhouette, refrigerator, advertisements

ANTARCTICA

Plus 1 Minus 1

separate, possess, exceed, cupboard, accurate, miniature, messenger, recognize, excerpt, rhythm, refrigerator, column, truly, chocolate, playwright, guard, rhyme, succeed, necessary, calendar, library, parallel, argument, suggest, arctic, guarantee, handsome, parliament, plague, accommodate, sieve, juice, doubt, guilty, receipt, lettuce

red, orange, yellow, green, blue, indigo, violet *(colours of the rainbow)*

Richard **O**f **Y**ork **G**ave **B**attle **I**n **V**ain

It's On The Tip Of My Tongue!

ambiguous, penultimate, paprika, curfew, surreal, panic, optimistic, Ramadan, truculent, carnivore, pessimist, trapezium, meticulous, cinnamon

Plus 1 Minus 1

address, label, foreigner, committee, eighth, espresso, amateur, until, manoeuvre, surprise, cinnamon, January, vacuum, disappeared, unskilful, irritable, satellite, tomorrow, believe, vegetable, definite, gauge, occasion, memento, pharaoh, advertise, disastrous, hamster, excellent, government, castles, fulfil, weird, yield

earth, Saturn, Jupiter, Venus, Mars, Mercury *(Uranus, Neptune and Pluto, which is a dwarf planet)*

Mister **V**incent **E**ats **M**ouldy **J**am **S**andwiches **U**nder **N**o **P**rotest

Pyramid Challenge!

ewe, pier, ocean, rhythm, library, deceived, rehearsal,
cautiously, rhododendron, choreographers,
conservationists, superstitiousness, uncharacteristically
DICTIONARY

Sound Alike!

dyed, grate, rowed, duel, storey, flair, board, plane, knight,
alter, ascent, through, passed
DADDY LONG LEGS

Jumble!

biscuit, llama, anemone, carousel, mississippi, weight,
hippopotamus, obelisk, chrysanthemum, giraffe, caffeine,
junction, refrigerator, principal
AUSTRALIA

Sound Alike!

guest, buoy, aisle, kneaded, healed, scent, whole, stairs,
maize, steel, role, bred
GOLDEN HAMSTER

Jumble!

daffodil, autumn, humorous, gateau, hospital, disguise,
clarinet, saucer, jewellery, elephant, Mediterranean,
cheetah, chemistry, physics, television
CALIFORNIA

Sound Alike!

lesson, style, serial, prophet, berth, draught, muscle
stationary, guilt, cymbal, chord, steak, hoard

Word For Word

horse + shore, shout + south, wrong + grown, chase +
aches, petal + plate, bream + amber, nectar + trance,
lemons + solemn, occurs + crocus, English + shingle,
outside + tedious, toaster + rotates, hardest + threads,
triangle + altering, organist + roasting, tiredness +
residents, galleries + allergies

RELATION/ORIENTAL

Confusables

1 effect/affect **2** canvass/canvas **3** practice/practise
4 dessert/desert **5** led/lead **6** licence/license **7** advice/
advise **8** proceed/precede **9** miner/minor **10** concur/
conquer

1 dependant/dependent **2** envelop/envelope **3** stationary/
stationery **4** council/counsel **5** eluded/alluded

Word Burgers

1 athletics **2** generally **3** medallist **4** maddening
5 carpenter **6** legendary **7** furniture **8** buccaneer
9 policeman **10** bellowing

LEAD PENCIL

Follow That Car!

caravan, caramel, cardigan, card, scarlet, caretaker, carnation, scarf, careful, scarecrow

At-TEN-tion!

tent, sentence, sweeten, frighten, tennis, tenor, mittens, kitten, listen, fastener, tenacious, christen

Word Burgers

1 volcanoes 2 shrinking 3 magnetism 4 obedience
5 defending 6 betraying 7 miserable 8 millipede
9 Halloween 10 splashing
CINDERELLA

Word Burgers

1 education 2 narrowest 3 opponents 4 sensitive
5 prisoners 6 operation 7 sprouting 8 spearmint
9 gardening 10 newsagent
CROSSROADS

Ants In Your Pants

servant, Canterbury, antler, panther, lantern, phantom, vacant, antique, giant, plant, tarantula, infant

Word For Word

canoe + ocean, lemon + melon, heart + earth,
table + bleat, elbow + below, peach + cheap,
hornet + throne, ascend + dances, dynamo + Monday,
kitchen + thicken, bedroom + boredom,
auction + caution, enlarge + general, oriental + relative,
sardines + aridness, orchestra + carthorse,
noiseless + lionesses
SUPERSONIC/PERCUSSION

Confusables

1 hanger/hangar 2 excess/access 3 premier/premiere
4 imminent/eminent 5 excerpt/exert 6 amid/among
7 device/devise 8 serial/cereal 9 accept/except

1 alternate/alternative 2 principal/principle 3 continual/
continuous 4 compliment/complement

Shh! Quiet Please!

1 wrong 2 knuckle 3 doubt 4 wrapper 5 column 6 wreath
7 science 8 honesty 9 gnaw 10 lamb 11 listen 12 whole
13 knock 14 thistle 15 gnat 16 crumbs 17 rustle 18 which
19 gnarled 20 solemn 21 plumber 22 muscle 23 gnu
24 scimitar 25 jostle
SCIENCE *(left out in Word Search)*

Heads and Tails

pear, pair, peel, peal, choir, agile, irate, piece, fringe, opaque, echoed, anchor, anxious, amateur, vehicle, fragile, ravenous, reliable, accurate, language, necessary, recognize, perpetual, permanent, nocturnal, conscious, hilarious

ARCHITECT

MAYONAISE *(answer in crossword grid)*

Starters

comprehend, commence, complex, complacent, combustion, comfortable, compliment, common, comedian, community, compact, compere, computer, combined harvester, compare, companion, commando, composer, comb, commuters, competent, comprehensive

Helps find north and south = **COMPASS**

Word Search

1 caramel **2** cartoon **3** carbon **4** caretaker **5** cardinal
6 carrot **7** career **8** cargo **9** carcass **10** careful
11 carnation **12** carpet **13** carpenter **14** cardigan **15** cardiac
16 carat **17** caravan **18** carafe **19** carefree **20** carnage
21 carp **22** carrion **23** carry **24** carton **25** carve **26** carol
27 cart **28** care

Starters

coral, cork, cordial, corny, corporal, corpuscle, corpse, corn, corrode, cornflower, cornea, corridor, cornet, cor anglais, corkscrew, correct, core, corner, cormorant, cord, coronet, corduroy

A royal crowning ceremony = **CORONATION**

Jumble!

conifer, moustache, pirates, waitress, surgeon, athletics, butterfly, astronomer, suggestion, slithered, astronaut, postponed, masculine, hibernated, supermarket

Heads and Tails

myth, debt, omit, hoax, queue, beige, debut, vinyl, rhythm, biased, absent, Israel, blatant, hygiene, deceive, arrived, calendar, punctual, diameter, argument, candidate, isosceles, volunteer, professor, sovereign, itinerary

CHAMELEON

LABORATORY (*answer in crossword grid*)

Shh! Quiet Please!

1 climb 2 thumb 3 knight 4 hymn 5 gnome 6 subtle
7 calm 8 honest 9 mistletoe 10 whistle 11 pneumonia
12 wrong 13 knowledge 14 gnashed 15 rhythm
16 pneumatic 17 scissors 18 castle 19 wreck
20 psychology 21 debt 22 wrist 23 ghost 24 wrinkle
25 receipt

SUBJECTS SPELLING LISTS

ART

abstract
adjective [**ab**-strakt] Abstract art is a style of art which uses shapes rather than images of people or objects.

acrylic [a-**kril**-lik]
noun Acrylics, or acrylic paints, are thick artists' paints which can be used like oil paints or thinned down with water.

architect [**ar**-kit-tekt]
noun A person who designs buildings.

architecture
noun The art or practice of designing buildings.

chalk
noun Chalk is a soft white rock. Small sticks of chalk are used for writing or drawing on a blackboard.

collage [**kol**-lahj]
noun A picture made by sticking pieces of paper or cloth onto a surface.

collection
noun A group of things acquired over a period of time • *A collection of paintings.*

colour
noun The appearance something has as a result of reflecting light.

crosshatching
noun Crosshatching is drawing an area of shade in a picture using two or more sets of parallel lines.

dimension
noun The dimensions of something are also its measurements, for example its length, breadth, height, or diameter.

display

verb An arrangement of things designed to attract people's attention.

easel

noun An upright frame which supports a picture that someone is painting.

exhibition

noun A public display of works of art, products, or skills.

foreground

noun In a picture, the foreground is the part that seems nearest.

frieze

noun A picture on a long strip of paper which is hung along a wall.

gallery

noun A building or room where works of art are shown.

Gothic

adjective **1** Gothic buildings have tall pillars, high vaulted ceilings, and pointed arches. **2** Gothic printing or writing has letters that are very ornate.

highlight

verb A lighter area of a painting, showing where light shines on things.

illusion

noun A false appearance of reality which deceives the eye

• *Painters create the illusion of space.*

impasto

noun A technique of painting with thick paint so that brush strokes or palette knife marks can be seen.

kiln

noun An oven for baking china or pottery until it becomes hard and dry.

landscape

noun A painting of the countryside.

neutral

adjective A neutral colour is not definite or striking, for example pale grey.

opus

noun An opus is a great artistic work, such as a piece of writing or a painting.

paint
noun Paint is a coloured liquid used to decorate buildings, or to make a picture.
verb If you paint something or paint a picture of it, you make a picture of it using paint.

palette
noun A palette is a flat piece of wood on which an artist mixes colours.

pastel
noun Pastels are small sticks of coloured crayon, used for drawing pictures.

pastiche [pass-**teesh**]
noun A pastiche is a work of art that contains a mixture of styles or that copies the style of another artist.

pencil
noun A long thin stick of wood with graphite in the centre, used for drawing or writing.

perspective
noun Perspective is a method artists use to make some people and things seem further away than others.

portrait
noun A picture or photograph of someone.

sketch
noun A quick, rough drawing.

spectrum
noun The spectrum is the range of different colours produced when light passes through a prism or a drop of water. A rainbow shows the colours in a spectrum.

surrealism
noun Surrealism began in the 1920s. It involves the putting together of strange images and things that are not normally seen together.

tone
noun A lighter, darker, or brighter shade of the same colour • *The whole room is painted in two tones of orange.*

D & T

aesthetic *or* **esthetic** [eess-**thet**-ik]
adjective Relating to the appreciation of beauty or art.

brief
verb When you brief someone on a task, you give them all the necessary instructions and information about it.

carbohydrate
noun Carbohydrate is a substance that gives you energy. It is found in foods like sugar and bread.

cell
noun A device that converts chemical energy to electricity.

Cellophane®
noun Cellophane® is thin, transparent plastic material used to wrap food or other things to protect them.

component
noun The components of something are the parts it is made of.

design
verb To design something means to plan it, especially by preparing a detailed sketch or drawings from which it can be built or made.
noun **1** A drawing or plan from which something can be built or made. **2** The design of something is its shape and style.

diet
noun **1** Someone's diet is the usual food that they eat • *A vegetarian diet.* **2** A special restricted selection of foods that someone eats to improve their health or regulate their weight.

disassemble
verb To disassemble a structure or object which has been made up or built from several smaller parts is to separate its parts from one another.

dowel
noun A dowel is a short, thin piece of wood or metal which is fitted into holes in larger pieces of wood or metal to join them together.

drawing pin
noun A drawing pin is a short nail with a broad, flat top.

drill
noun A tool for making holes • *An electric drill.*

verb To drill into something means to make a hole in it using a drill.

evaluation
noun To carry out an evaluation of a design, product or system is to do an assessment to find out how well it works or will work.

fabric
noun **1** Cloth • *Tough fabric for tents.* **2** The fabric of a building is its walls, roof, and other parts.

felt
noun Felt is a thick cloth made by pressing short threads together.

fibre
noun A thin thread of a substance used to make cloth.

fibreglass
noun Fibreglass is a material made from thin threads of glass. It can be mixed with plastic to make boats, cars, and furniture, and is often used as an insulating material.

file
noun A long steel tool with a rough surface, used for smoothing and shaping hard materials.

finish
noun The finish that something has is the texture or appearance of its surface • *A healthy, glossy finish.*

flavour
noun **1** The flavour of food is its taste. **2** The flavour of something is its distinctive characteristic or quality.
verb If you flavour food with a spice or herb, you add it to the food to give it a particular taste.

flour
noun Flour is a powder made from finely ground grain, usually wheat, and used for baking and cooking.

flow chart
noun A diagram showing the sequence of steps that lead to various results.

foam
noun Foam is light spongy material used, for example, in furniture or packaging.

fulcrum
noun The point at which something is balancing or pivoting.

gear
noun A piece of machinery which controls the rate at which energy is converted into movement. Gears in vehicles control the speed and power of the vehicle.

hygiene [**high**-jeen]
noun Hygiene is the practice of keeping yourself and your surroundings clean, especially to stop the spread of disease.

ingredient
noun Ingredients are the things that something is made from, especially in cookery.

innovation
noun A completely new idea, product, or system of doing things.

joint
noun A place where two things are fixed together.

knife
noun A sharp metal tool that you use to cut things.

linen
noun Linen is a type of cloth made from a plant called flax.

machine
noun A piece of equipment which uses electricity or power from an engine to make it work.

manufacture
verb To manufacture goods is to make them in a factory.
noun The manufacture of goods is the making of them in a factory
• *The manufacture of nuclear weapons.*

marketing
noun Marketing is the part of a business concerned with the way a product is sold.

market research
noun Market research is research into what people want and buy.

material
noun **1** Material is cloth. **2** A substance from which something is made • *The materials to make red dye.* **3** The equipment for a particular activity can be referred to as materials • *building materials.*

mechanism
noun A part of a machine that does a particular task • *A locking mechanism.*

mineral
noun A substance such as tin, salt, or coal that is formed naturally in rocks and in the earth • *Rich mineral deposits.*

monorail
noun A monorail is a railway running on a single rail usually raised above ground level.

motor
noun A part of a vehicle or a machine that uses electricity or fuel to produce movement so that the machine can work.
adjective Concerned with or relating to vehicles with a petrol or diesel engine • *The motor industry.*

mould
verb To mould a substance is to make it into a particular shape • *Mould the mixture into flat round cakes.*
noun A container used to make something into a particular shape • *A jelly mould.*

natural
adjective Existing or happening in nature • *Natural gas.*

neutral
adjective The neutral wire in an electric plug is the one that is not earth or live.
noun Neutral is the position between the gears of a vehicle in which the gears are not connected to the engine and so the vehicle cannot move.

nutrition
noun Nutrition is the food that you eat, considered from the point of view of how it helps you to grow and remain healthy • *The effects of poor nutrition are evident.*

packaging
noun Packaging is the container or wrapping in which an item is sold or sent.

pneumatic [new-**mat**-ik]
adjective Operated by or filled with compressed air • *A pneumatic drill.*

polyester
noun A man-made fibre, used especially to make clothes.

presentation
noun To give a presentation is to give a talk or demonstration to an audience of something you have been studying or working on.

production

noun **1** Production is the process of manufacturing or growing something in large quantities • *Modern methods of production.*
2 Production is also the amount of goods manufactured or food grown by a country or company • *Production has fallen by 13.2%.*

protein

noun Protein is a substance that is found in meat, eggs, and milk and that is needed by bodies for growth.

prototype

noun A first model of something that is made so that the design can be tested and improved.

pulley

noun A device for lifting heavy weights. The weight is attached to a rope which passes over a wheel or series of wheels.

recipe [**res**-sip-ee]

noun **1** A list of ingredients and instructions for cooking something. **2** If something is a recipe for disaster or for success, it is likely to result in disaster or success.

sandpaper

noun Sandpaper is strong paper with a coating of sand on it, used for rubbing surfaces to make them smooth.

scissors

plural noun Scissors are a cutting tool with two sharp blades.

sew [so]

verb When you sew things together, you join them using a needle and thread.

shaft

noun A shaft in a machine is a rod which revolves and transfers movement in the machine • *The drive shaft.*

sheet

noun A sheet of glass or metal is a large, flat piece of it.

specification

noun A detailed description of what is needed for something, such as the necessary features in the design of something • *I like to build it to my own specifications.*

stiff

adjective Something that is stiff is firm and not easily bent.

structure
noun The structure of something is the way it is made, built, or organized.
verb To structure something means to arrange it into an organized pattern or system.

technology
noun Technology is the study of the application of science and scientific knowledge for practical purposes in industry, farming, medicine, or business.

tension
noun The tension in a rope or wire is how tightly it is stretched.

textile
noun A woven cloth or fabric.

transparent
adjective If something is transparent, you can see through it.

vitamin
noun Vitamins are organic compounds which you need in order to remain healthy. They occur naturally in food.

wheel
noun **1** A circular object which turns on a rod attached to its centre. Wheels are fixed underneath vehicles so that they can move along. **2** The wheel of a car is its steering wheel.

wire
verb If you wire something or wire it up, you connect it so that electricity can pass through it.

yarn
noun Yarn is thread used for knitting or making cloth.

DRAMA

applause
noun Applause is clapping by a group of people.

costume
noun A set of clothes worn by an actor.

curtain
noun A large piece of material which hangs in front of the stage in a theatre until a performance begins.

director
noun The person responsible for the making and performance of a programme, play, or film.

dramatist
noun A person who writes plays.

entrance [**en**-trunss]
noun In the theatre, an actor makes his or her entrance when he or she comes on to the stage.

exit
verb An actor exits when he or she leaves the stage.

freeze
verb To freeze the action in a film is to stop the film at a particular frame.

improvise
verb When actors improvise, they make up the words as they go along.

inspire
verb If something inspires you, it gives you new ideas and enthusiasm to do something.

lighting
noun Lighting in the theatre or for a film is the special lights that are directed on the performers or scene.

movement
noun Movement involves changing position or going from one place to another.

perform
verb To perform is to act, dance, or play music in front of an audience.

performance
noun An entertainment provided for an audience.

playwright
noun A person who writes plays.

position
noun The position of someone or something is the place where they are or ought to be • *Would the cast take their positions, please.*

rehearsal
noun A practice of a performance in preparation for the actual event.

rehearse
verb To rehearse a performance means to practise it in preparation for the actual event.

role
noun An actor's role is the character that he or she plays • *her first leading role.*

scenario [sin-**nar**-ee-oh]
noun The scenario of a film or play is a summary of its plot.

scene
noun Part of a play or film in which a series of events happen in one place.

script
noun The written version of a play or film.

share
verb If you share an idea or a piece of news with someone, you tell it to them.

spotlight
noun A powerful light which can be directed to light up a small area.

stage
noun **1** In a theatre, the stage is a raised platform where the actors or entertainers perform. **2** You can refer to the profession of acting as the stage.

theatre [**thee**-uh-tuh]
noun **1** A building where plays and other entertainments are performed on a stage. **2** Theatre is work such as writing, producing, and acting in plays.

theatrical [thee-**at**-rik-kl]
adjective Involving the theatre or performed in a theatre • *His theatrical career.*

ENGLISH

accent
noun Stress placed on a particular word, syllable, or note.

adjective
noun A word that adds to the description given by a noun. For

example, in 'They live in a large white Georgian house', 'large', 'white', and 'Georgian' are all adjectives.

adverb

noun A word that adds information about a verb or a following adjective or other adverb, for example, 'slowly', 'now', and 'here' which say how, when, or where something is done.

advertise

verb **1** If you advertise something, you tell people about it in a newspaper or poster, or on TV. **2** To advertise is to make an announcement in a newspaper or poster, or on TV.

advertisement [ad-**ver**-tiss-ment]

noun An announcement about something in a newspaper or poster, or on TV.

alliteration

noun The use of several words together which all begin with the same sound, for example 'around the ragged rock the ragged rascal ran'.

allusion

noun An indirect reference to or comment about something
• *English literature is full of classical allusions.*

apostrophe [ap-**poss**-troff-ee]

noun A punctuation mark used to show that one or more letters have been missed out of a word, for example "he's" for "he is". Apostrophes are also used with -s at the end of a noun to show that what follows belongs to or relates to the noun, for example *my brother's books*. If the noun already has an -s at the end, for example because it is plural, you just add the apostrophe, eg *my brothers' books*, referring to more than one brother.

assonance

noun The use of similar vowel or consonant sounds in words near to each other or in the same word, for example 'a long storm'.

atmosphere

noun The mood created by the writer of a novel or play.

author

noun The author of a book is the person who wrote it.

ballad

noun A long song or poem which tells a story.

character
noun The characters in a film, play, or book are the people in it.

clause
noun In grammar, a clause is a group of words with a subject and a verb, which may be a complete sentence or one of the parts of a sentence.

cliché [**klee**-shay]
noun An idea or phrase which is no longer effective because it has been used so much.

climax
noun The climax of a process, story, or piece of music is the most exciting moment in it, usually near the end.

comma
noun The punctuation mark (,).

comparison
noun When you make a comparison, you consider two things together and see in what ways they are different or similar.

conjugate [**kon**-joo-gate]
verb When you conjugate a verb, you list the different forms of it you use with the pronouns 'I', 'you' (singular), 'he', 'she', 'it', 'you' (plural), and 'they'.

conjunction
noun In grammar, a conjunction is a word that links two other words or two clauses, for example 'and', 'but', 'while', and 'that'.

connotation
noun The connotations of a word or name are what it makes you think of • *A grey man for whom grey has no connotation of dullness.*

consonant
noun A sound such as 'p' or 'm' which you make by stopping the air flowing freely through your mouth.

context
noun The context of a word or sentence consists of the words or sentences before and after it.

contraction
noun A shortened form of a word or words, for example *I'm* for *I am*.

couplet
noun Two lines of poetry together, especially two that rhyme.

determiner
noun A word that can go before a noun or noun group to show, for instance, which thing you are referring to or whether you are referring to one thing or several. For example, in 'my house', 'the windows', 'this red book', and 'each time', 'my', 'the', 'this', and 'each' can be called determiners.

dialogue
noun In a novel, play, or film, dialogue is conversation.

diphthong
noun A diphthong is a vowel in which the speaker's tongue changes position while it is being pronounced, so that the vowel sounds like a combination of two other vowels.

direct speech
noun The reporting of what someone has said by quoting the exact words.

discursive
adjective In English, a discursive essay reaches its conclusion through reasoning and argument rather than intuition.

edition
noun An edition of a book or magazine is a particular version of it printed at one time.

ellipsis
noun Ellipsis is the omission of parts of a sentence when the sentence can be understood without these parts. An example is 'You coming too?', where 'Are' has been omitted from the beginning of the question.

enjambment *or* enjambement [in-**jam**-ment]
noun In poetry, enjambment is when a sentence or phrase runs from one line of verse over to the next without a pause between lines.

epilogue [**ep**-ill-og]
noun An epilogue is a passage added to the end of a book or play as a conclusion.

episode
noun One of several parts of a novel or drama appearing for example on television ● *I never miss an episode of 'Neighbours'.*

etymology [et-tim-**ol**-loj-ee]
noun Etymology is the study of the origin and changes of form in words.

exclamation
noun A word or phrase spoken suddenly to express a strong feeling.

expression
noun The expression of ideas or feelings is the showing of them through words, actions, or art.

figurative
adjective If you use a word or expression in a figurative sense, you use it with a more abstract or imaginative meaning than its ordinary one.

figure of speech
noun A figure of speech is an expression such as a simile or idiom in which the words are not used in their literal sense.

first person
noun In English grammar, the first person is the 'I' or 'we' form of the pronoun or the verb.

first-person narrator
noun A first-person narrator is the principal character in a story and uses the pronoun *I*.

genre [jahn-ra]
noun A particular style in literature or art.

grammar
noun Grammar is the rules of a language relating to the ways you can combine words to form sentences.

haiku
noun A type of very short Japanese poem which has 17 syllables.

homonym
noun Homonyms are words which are pronounced or spelt in the same way but which have different meanings. For example, *swift* is an adjective meaning 'fast', and the name for a type of bird; *meat* is the flesh of animals, and *meet* is a verb meaning 'encounter'.

homophone
noun Homophones are words with different meanings which are pronounced in the same way but are spelt differently. For example, 'write' and 'right' are homophones.

iambic
adjective If a line of verse is iambic, it is made up of rhythmic units

called *iambs*, which have one unstressed syllable followed by a stressed one.

imagery

noun The imagery of a poem or book is the descriptive language used in it.

introduction

noun A piece of writing at the beginning of a book, which usually tells you what the book is about.

irony [**eye**-ron-ee]

noun **1** Irony is a form of humour in which you say the opposite of what you really mean • *This group could be described, without irony, as the fortunate ones.* **2** There is irony in a situation when there is an unexpected or unusual connection between things or events • *It's a sad irony of life: once you are lost, a map is useless.*

literal

adjective **1** The literal meaning of a word is its most basic meaning. **2** A literal translation from a foreign language is one that has been translated exactly word for word.

literature

noun Literature consists of novels, plays, and poetry.

memoirs [**mem**-wahrz]

plural noun If someone writes their memoirs, they write a book about their life and experiences.

metaphor

noun An imaginative way of describing something as another thing, and so suggesting that it has the typical qualities of that other thing. For example, if you wanted to say that someone is shy, you might say they are a mouse.

metre

noun In poetry, metre is the regular and rhythmic arrangement of words and syllables.

mnemonic [nim-**on**-nik]

noun A mnemonic is a word or rhyme that helps you to remember things such as scientific facts or spelling rules. 'i before e, except after c' is an example of a mnemonic.

monologue [**mon**-nol-og]

noun A long speech by one person during a play or a conversation.

myth
 noun A story which was made up long ago to explain natural events and religious beliefs • *Viking myths.*

narrative [**nar**-rat-tiv]
 noun A story or an account of events.

narrator
 noun A character in a novel who tells the story.

noun
 noun A word which refers to a person, thing, or idea. Examples of nouns are 'president', 'table', 'sun', and 'beauty'.

ode
 noun A poem written in praise of someone or something.

omniscient narrator
 noun A narrator who tells a story that he or she is not part of, and who knows everything about all the characters: their past, their future, and even what they think.

onomatopoeia [on-o-mat-o-**pee**-a]
 noun The use of words which sound like the thing that they represent. 'Hiss' and 'buzz' are examples of onomatopoeia.

oxymoron
 noun Two words that contradict each other placed beside each other, for example 'deafening silence'.

palindrome
 noun A palindrome is a word or phrase that is the same whether you read it forwards or backwards; for example the word 'refer'.

pamphlet
 noun A very thin book in paper covers giving information about something.

paragraph
 noun A section of a piece of writing. Paragraphs begin on a new line.

passive
 noun In grammar, the passive or passive voice is the form of the verb in which the person or thing to which an action is being done is the grammatical subject of the sentence, and is given more emphasis as a result. For example, the passive of *The committee rejected your application* is *Your application was rejected by the committee.*

past participle

noun In grammar, the past participle of an English verb is the form, usually ending in '-ed' or '-en', that is used to make some past tenses and the passive. For example 'killed' in 'She has killed the goldfish' and 'broken' in 'My leg was broken' are past participles.

perfect

adjective In English grammar, the perfect tense of a verb is formed with the present tense of 'have' and the past participle of the main verb • *I have lost my home.*

personification

noun Personification is a form of imagery in which something inanimate is described as if it has human qualities • *The trees sighed and whispered as the impatient breeze stirred their branches.*

playwright

noun A person who writes plays.

plot

noun The plot of a novel or play is the story.

plural

noun The form of a word that is used to refer to two or more people or things, for example the plural of 'chair' is 'chairs', and the plural of 'mouse' is 'mice'.

poetic licence

noun If a writer or poet uses poetic licence, they change the facts or the usual rules to make what they are writing more powerful or interesting.

prefix

noun A letter or group of letters added to the beginning of a word to make a new word, for example 'semi-', 'pre-', and 'un-'.

preposition

noun A word such as 'by', 'for', 'into', or 'with', which usually has a noun as its object.

pronoun

noun In grammar, a pronoun is a word that is used to replace a noun. 'He', 'she', and 'them' are all pronouns.

pronounce

verb When you pronounce a word, you say it.

punctuation
noun The marks in writing such as full stops, question marks, and commas are called punctuation or punctuation marks.

repetition
noun Repetition is when a word, phrase, or sound is repeated, for example to emphasize a point or to make sure it is understood, or for poetic effect.

resolution
noun The resolution of a problem is the solving of it.

rhyme
verb If two words rhyme, they have a similar sound • *Sally rhymes with valley.*
noun A short poem with rhyming lines.

root word
noun A root word is a word from which other words can be made by adding a suffix or a prefix. For example, *clearly* and *unclear* can be made from the root word *clear.*

scene [seen]
noun Part of a play or film in which a series of events happen in one place.

second person
noun In grammar, the second person is the person being spoken to (*you*).

second-person narrator
noun A second-person narrator addresses the reader directly using the pronoun *you* and tells a story as if the reader is the character whose thoughts and actions are being described. For example, a **second-person narrative** might begin 'You are standing in a dusty street, pretending to be doing nothing...'

sentimental
adjective Sentimental literature is intended to provoke an emotional response to the story, rather than relying on the reader's own natural response.

simile [sim-ill-ee]
noun An expression in which a person or thing is described as being similar to someone or something else. Examples of similes are *She runs like a deer* and *He's as white as a sheet.*

soliloquy [sol-**lill**-ok-wee]
noun A speech in a play made by a character who is alone on the stage.

sonnet
noun A poem with 14 lines, in which lines rhyme according to fixed patterns.

split infinitive
noun A split infinitive is an infinitive with a word between the 'to' and the verb, as in 'to boldly go'. This is often thought to be incorrect.

stanza
noun A verse of a poem.

stress
noun Stress is emphasis put on a word or part of a word when it is pronounced, making it slightly louder.

suffix
noun A group of letters which is added to the end of a word to form a new word, for example '-ology' or '-itis'.

syllable
noun A part of a word that contains a single vowel sound and is pronounced as a unit. For example, 'book' has one syllable and 'reading' has two.

synonym
noun If two words have the same or a very similar meaning, they are synonyms.

syntax
noun The syntax of a language is its grammatical rules and the way its words are arranged.

tabloid
noun A newspaper with small pages, short news stories, and lots of photographs.

tautology
noun Tautology is using different words to say the same thing twice in the same sentence.

third person
noun In grammar, the third person is anyone or anything being referred to which isn't a first or second person (*he*, *she*, *they*, or *it*).

third-person narrator
noun A third-person narrator is either a minor character in the story or not a character at all and uses the pronouns *he*, *she*, *it*, and *they*.

tone
noun The tone of a piece of writing is its style and the ideas or opinions expressed in it • *I was shocked at the tone of your leading article.*

verb
noun In grammar, a verb is a word that expresses actions and states, for example 'be', 'become', 'take', and 'run'.

vocabulary
noun **1** Someone's vocabulary is the total number of words they know in a particular language. **2** The vocabulary of a language is all the words in it.

vowel
noun A sound made without your tongue touching the roof of your mouth or your teeth, or one of the letters a, e, i, o, u, which represent such sounds.

wordplay
noun Wordplay is the making of jokes by clever use of words

GEOGRAPHY

abroad
adverb In a foreign country.

altitude
noun The altitude of something is its height above sea level • *The mountain range reaches an altitude of 1330 metres.*

amenity [am-**mee**-nit-ee]
noun Amenities are things that are available for the public to use, such as sports facilities or shopping centres.

atlas
noun A book of maps.

authority
noun In Britain, an authority is a local government department • *Local health authorities.*

climate

noun The climate of a place is the typical weather conditions there • *The climate was dry in the summer.*

contour

noun On a map, a contour is a line joining points of equal height.

country

noun One of the political areas the world is divided into.

county

noun A region with its own local government.

current

noun **1** A strong continuous movement of the water in a river or in the sea. **2** An air current is a flowing movement in the air.

desert [**dez**-ert]

noun A region of land with very little plant life, usually because of low rainfall.

employment

noun Employment is the state of having a paid job, or the activity of recruiting people for a job.

erosion

noun The gradual wearing away and destruction of something • *Soil erosion.*

estuary [**est**-yoo-ree]

noun The wide part of a river near where it joins the sea and where fresh water mixes with salt water.

fauna [**faw**-na]

noun The fauna of a particular area is all the animals found in that area • *The flora and fauna of Africa.*

fertilizer *or* fertiliser

noun A substance put onto soil to improve plant growth.

global warming

noun An increase in the world's overall temperature believed to be caused by the greenhouse effect.

globe

noun You can refer to the world as the globe.

greenhouse effect

noun The gradual rise in temperature in the earth's atmosphere due to heat being absorbed from the sun and being trapped by gases such as carbon dioxide in the air around the earth.

habitat
noun The natural home of a plant or animal.

hurricane
noun A hurricane is a violent wind or storm, usually force 12 or above on the Beaufort scale.

infrastructure
noun The infrastructure of a country consists of things like factories, schools, and roads, which show how much money the country has and how strong its economy is.

international
adjective Involving different countries.

landscape
noun The landscape is the view over an area of open land.

latitude
noun The latitude of a place is its distance north or south of the equator measured in degrees.

lava
noun Lava is the very hot liquid rock that comes shooting out of an erupting volcano, and becomes solid as it cools.

location
noun A place, or the position of something.

longitude
noun The longitude of a place is its distance east or west of a line passing through Greenwich, measured in degrees.

nation
noun A large group of people sharing the same history and language and usually inhabiting a particular country.

national
adjective **1** Relating to the whole of a country • *A national newspaper.* **2** Typical of a particular country • *Women in Polish national dress.*
noun A national of a country is a citizen of that country • *Turkish nationals.*

natural resources
plural noun Materials such as minerals, trees, coal etc. that exist naturally in a country and can be used by its people.

North Pole
   noun The North Pole is the most northerly point of the earth's surface.

physical
   adjective Relating to things that can be touched or seen, especially with regard to their size or shape • *The physical characteristics of their machinery* • *The physical world.*

pollution
   noun Pollution of the environment happens when dirty or dangerous substances get into the air, water, or soil.

poverty
   noun The state of being very poor.

precipitation
   noun Precipitation is rain, snow, or hail; used especially when stating the amount that falls during a particular period.

provision
   noun **1** The provision of something is the act of making it available to people • *The provision of health care.* **2** (in plural) Provisions are supplies of food.

region
   noun A large area of land.

rural
   adjective Relating to or involving the countryside.

settlement
   noun A place where people have settled and built homes.

situation
   noun The situation of a building or town is its surroundings • *A beautiful situation.*

stalactite
   noun A stalactite is a piece of rock like a huge icicle hanging from the roof of a cave.

stalagmite
   noun A stalagmite is a large pointed piece of rock sticking up from the floor of a cave.

tourism
   noun Tourism is the business of providing services for people on holiday, for example hotels and sightseeing trips.

tourist
noun A person who visits places for pleasure or interest.

transport
noun Vehicles that you travel in are referred to as transport
• *Public transport.*
verb When goods or people are transported from one place to another, they are moved there.

transportation
noun Transportation is the transporting of people and things from one place to another.

urban
adjective Relating to a town or city • *She found urban life very different to country life.*

wealth
noun Wealth is the large amount of money or property which someone owns.

weather
noun The weather is the condition of the atmosphere at any particular time and the amount of rain, wind, or sunshine occurring.
verb If something such as rock or wood weathers, it changes colour or shape as a result of being exposed to the wind, rain, or sun.

HISTORY

agriculture
noun Agriculture is farming.

bias
noun Someone who shows bias favours one person or thing unfairly.

blitz
noun A bombing attack by enemy aircraft on a city.
verb When a city is blitzed, it is bombed by aircraft and is damaged or destroyed.

castle
noun A large building with walls or ditches round it to protect it from attack.

cathedral
noun An important church with a bishop in charge of it.

Catholic
adjective Relating or belonging to the branch of the Christian church that accepts the Pope in Rome as its leader.
noun Someone who belongs to the Roman Catholic church.

chronological [kron-nol-**loj**-i-kl]
adjective Arranged in the order in which things happened • *Tell me the whole story in chronological order.*

chronology [kron-**nol**-loj-jee]
noun The chronology of events is the order in which they happened.

citizen
noun The citizens of a country or city are the people who live in it or belong to it • *American citizens.*

civilization *or* civilisation
noun **1** A society which has a highly developed organization and culture • *The tale of a lost civilization.* **2** Civilization is an advanced state of social organization and culture.

colonize *or* colonise
verb When people colonize a place, they go to live there and take control of it • *The Europeans who colonized North America.*

colony
noun **1** A country controlled by a more powerful country. **2** A group of people who settle in a country controlled by their homeland.

conflict
noun [**kon**-flikt] A war or battle.

constitution
noun The constitution of a country is the system of laws which formally states people's rights and duties.

contradict
verb If you contradict someone, you say that what they have just said is not true, and that something else is.

current
noun Something that is current is happening, being done, or being used now.

defence
noun A country's defences are its military resources, such as its armed forces and weapons.

disease
noun An unhealthy condition in people, animals, or plants.

document
noun A piece of paper which provides an official record of something.
verb If you document something, you make a detailed record of it.

dynasty
noun A series of rulers of a country all belonging to the same family.

economic(al)
adjective Concerning the management of the money, industry, and trade of a country.

economy
noun The economy of a country is the system it uses to organize and manage its money, industry, and trade; also used of the wealth that a country gets from business and industry.

emigration
noun Emigration is the process of emigrating, especially by large numbers of people at various periods of history.

government
noun **1** The government is the group of people who govern a country. **2** The control and organization of a country.

immigrant
noun Someone who has come to live permanently in a new country.

imperial
adjective Imperial means relating to an empire or an emperor or empress • *The Imperial Palace.*

imperialism
noun A system of rule in which a rich and powerful nation controls other nations.

independence
noun A nation or state gains its independence when it stops being ruled or governed by another country and has its own government and laws.

invasion
> *noun* The invasion of a country or territory is the act of entering it by force.

king
> *noun* A man who is the head of state in a country, and who inherited his position from his parents.

motive
> *noun* A reason or purpose for doing something • *There was no motive for the attack.*

Neanderthal [nee-**an**-der-tahl]
> *adjective* Neanderthal man was a primitive species of man who lived in Europe before 12,000 BC. The name comes from Neandertal, a German valley where archaeological discoveries were made.

parliament
> *noun* The group of elected representatives who make the laws of a country.

politics
> *noun* Politics is the activity and planning concerned with achieving power and control in a country or organization.

propaganda
> *noun* Propaganda is exaggerated or false information that is published or broadcast in order to influence people.

Protestant
> *adjective* Relating or belonging to one of the Christian Churches that separated from the Catholic Church in the sixteenth century.
> *noun* Someone who belongs to one of these churches.

rebel
> *noun* [**reh**-bl] Rebels are people who are fighting their own country's army to change the political system.
> *verb* [reh-**bel**] To rebel means to fight against authority and reject accepted values.

rebellion
> *noun* A rebellion is organized and often violent opposition to authority.

reign [rain]
> *noun* The reign of a king or queen is the period during which he or she reigns.

religious
adjective Connected with religion • *religious worship.*

revolt
noun A violent attempt by a group of people to change their country's political system.
verb When people revolt, they fight against the authority that governs them.

revolution
noun **1** A violent attempt by a large group of people to change the political system of their country. **2** An important change in an area of human activity • *The Industrial Revolution.*

siege [seej]
noun A siege is a military operation in which an army surrounds a place and prevents food or help from reaching the people inside.

source
noun A source is a person or book that provides information for a news story or for research.

trade
noun Trade is the activity of buying, selling, or exchanging goods or services between people, firms, or countries.

traitor
noun Someone who betrays their country or the group which they belong to.

ICT

binary [by-nar-ee]
adjective The binary system expresses numbers using only two digits, 0 and 1.

byte
noun A unit of storage in a computer.

data
noun Any information put into a computer and which the computer works on or processes.

database
noun A collection of information stored in a computer.

delete
verb To delete something means to cross it out or remove it • *He had deleted the computer file by mistake.*

disk *or* **disc**
noun In a computer, the disk is the part where information is stored.

document
noun A piece of text or graphics stored in a computer as a file that can be amended or altered by document processing software.

download
verb If you download data you transfer it from the memory of one computer to that of another, especially over the Internet.
noun A piece of data transferred in this way.

electronic
adjective Having transistors or silicon chips which control an electric current.

graphics
plural noun Graphics are drawings and pictures composed of simple lines and strong colours • *Computerized graphics.*

hardware
noun Hardware is also computer machinery rather than computer programs.

icon [**eye**-kon]
noun A picture on a computer screen representing a program that can be activated by moving the cursor over it.

input
noun In computing, input is information which is fed into a computer.

interactive
adjective Interactive television, computers and games react to decisions taken by the viewer, user or player.

interface
noun The user interface of a computer program is how it is presented on the computer screen and how easy it is to operate.

Internet
noun The Internet is a worldwide communication system which people use through computers.

justify
verb To justify text that you have typed or keyed into a computer

is to adjust the spaces between the words so each full line in a paragraph fills the space between the left and right hand margins of the page.

keyboard
noun A row of levers or buttons on a piano, typewriter, or computer.

megabyte
noun A unit of storage in a computer, equal to 1,048,576 bytes.

memory
noun The part in which information is stored in a computer.

modem [moe-dem]
noun A piece of equipment that links a computer to the telephone system so that data can be transferred from one machine to another via the telephone line.

module
noun A part of a machine or system that does a particular task.

monitor
noun The visual display unit of a computer.

mouse
noun A small device moved by hand to control the position of the cursor on a computer screen.

multimedia
noun In computing, you use multimedia to refer to products which use sound, pictures, film and ordinary text to convey information.

network
noun A group of computers connected to each other.

output
noun The output of a computer is the information it produces.

password
noun A word you need to know to get into some computers or computer files.

preview
noun A part of a computer program which allows you to look at what you have keyed or added to a document or spreadsheet as it will appear when it is printed.

processor
noun In computing, a processor is the central chip in a computer which controls its operations.

program
noun A set of instructions that a computer follows to perform a particular task.
verb When someone programs a computer, they write a program and put it into the computer.

RAM
noun A storage space which can be filled with data but which loses its contents when the machine is switched off. RAM stands for 'random access memory'.

ROM
noun ROM is a storage device that holds data permanently and cannot be altered by the programmer. ROM stands for 'read only memory'.

scanner
noun A machine which converts text or images into a form that can be stored on a computer.

sensor
noun An instrument which reacts to physical conditions such as light or heat.

server
noun A computer or computer program which supplies information or resources to a number of computers on a network.

software
noun Computer programs are known as software.

spreadsheet
noun A computer program that is used for entering and arranging figures, used mainly for financial planning.

virus [**vie**-russ]
noun A program that alters or damages the information stored in a computer system

LIBRARY

alphabet
noun A set of letters in a fixed order that is used in writing a language.

anthology
noun A collection of writings by various authors published in one book.

article
noun A piece of writing in a newspaper or magazine.

catalogue
noun A list of things such as the objects in a museum or the books in a library.

classify
verb To classify things is to arrange them into groups with similar characteristics.

content
noun [**con**-tent] The content of an article or speech is what is expressed in it.

copyright
noun If someone has the copyright on a piece of writing or music, it cannot be copied or performed without their permission.

dictionary
noun A book in which words are listed alphabetically and explained, or equivalent words are given in another language.

editor
noun **1** A person who is responsible for the content of a newspaper or magazine. **2** A person who checks books and makes corrections to them before they are published.

encyclopedia *or* encyclopaedia [en-sigh-klop-**ee**-dee-a]
noun A book or set of books giving information about many different subjects.

extract
noun A small section taken from a book or piece of music.

fantasy
noun In books and films, fantasy is the people or situations in books or films which are created in the writer's imagination and do not reflect reality.

genre [**jahn**-ra]
noun A particular style in literature or art.

glossary
noun A list of explanations of specialist words, usually found at the back of a book.

index

noun An index is also a set of cards listing all the books in a library, arranged alphabetically.

irrelevant

adjective Not directly connected with a subject ● *He either ignored questions or gave irrelevant answers.*

librarian

noun A person who works in, or is in charge of, a library.

magazine

noun A weekly or monthly publication with articles and photographs.

nonfiction

noun Nonfiction is writing that gives facts and information rather than telling a story.

novel

noun A book that tells an invented story.

photocopy

noun A copy of a document produced by a photocopier.
verb If you photocopy a document, you make a copy of it using a photocopier.

publisher

noun The publisher of a book, newspaper or magazine is the person or company that prints copies of it and distributes it.

relevant

adjective If something is relevant, it is connected with and is appropriate to what is being discussed ● *We have passed all relevant information on to the police.*

romance

noun A novel about a love affair.

series

noun A series of things is a number of them coming one after the other.

system

noun An organized way of doing or arranging something according to a fixed plan or set of rules.

thesaurus [this-**saw**-russ]

noun A reference book in which words with similar meanings are grouped together.

MATHEMATICS

addition
noun The process of adding numbers together.

adjacent [ad-**jay**-sent]
adjective Adjacent angles share one side and have the same point opposite to their bases.

alternate
adjective [ol-**tern**-at] Alternate angles are two angles on opposite sides of a line that crosses two other lines.

amount
noun An amount of something is how much there is of it.

angle
noun The distance between two lines at the point where they join together. Angles are measured in degrees.

approximate
adjective Almost exact • *What was the approximate distance?*

area
noun The area of a geometric object is the amount of space enclosed within its lines.

average
noun A result obtained by adding several amounts together and then dividing the total by the number of different amounts • *Six pupils were examined in a total of 39 subjects, an average of 6.5 subjects per pupil.*

axis [**ak**-siss]
noun One of the two sides of a graph.

calculate
verb If you calculate something, you work it out, usually by doing some arithmetic.

centimetre
noun A unit of length equal to ten millimetres or one hundredth of a metre.

circumference
noun The circumference of a circle is its outer line or edge; also the length of this line.

coordinate [koh-**or**-din-ate]
plural noun Coordinates are a pair of numbers or letters which tell you how far along and up or down a point is on a grid.

corresponding angle

noun Corresponding angles occur where a line crosses two or more parallel lines. They are the equivalent angles on the same side of the intersection.

decimal

adjective The decimal system expresses numbers using all the digits from 0 to 9.

noun A fraction in which a dot called a decimal point is followed by numbers representing tenths, hundredths, and thousandths. For example, 0.5 represents $^5/_{10}$ (or ½); 0.05 represents $^5/_{100}$ (or $^1/_{20}$).

degree

noun A unit of measurement of angles in mathematics, and of latitude and longitude.

denominator

noun In maths, the denominator is the bottom part of a fraction.

diameter

noun The diameter of a circle is the length of a straight line drawn across it through its centre.

digit [**dij**-it]

noun A written symbol for any of the numbers from 0 to 9.

divide

verb In mathematics, when you divide, you calculate how many times one number contains another.

equilateral

adjective An equilateral triangle has sides that are all the same length.

estimate

noun A guess at an amount, quantity, or outcome, based on the evidence you have available.

fraction

noun In arithmetic, a fraction is a part of a whole number. A **proper fraction** is a fraction in which the number above the line is lower than the number below it; an **improper fraction** has the greater number above the line • *3/4 is a proper fraction.*

graph

noun A diagram in which a line shows how two sets of numbers or measurements are related.

guess
verb If you guess something, you form or express an opinion that it is the case, without having much information.
noun A guess is an attempt to give the correct answer to something without having much information, or without working it out properly.

hexagon
noun A shape with six straight sides; a **regular hexagon** has six straight sides of the same length.

horizontal [hor-riz-**zon**-tl]
adjective Flat and parallel with the horizon or with a line considered as a base • *A patchwork of vertical and horizontal black lines.*

isosceles [eye-**soss**-il-eez]
adjective An isosceles triangle has two sides of the same length.

kilogram
noun A kilogram is a unit of weight equal to 1000 grams.

kilometre
noun A unit of distance equal to one thousand metres.

litre
noun A unit of liquid volume equal to about 1.76 pints.

measure
verb When you measure something, you find out how big it is.

metre
noun The metre is the SI unit of length. One metre is equal to 100 centimetres.

minus You use 'minus' to show that one number is being subtracted from another • *Ten minus six equals four.*

multiply
verb When you multiply one number by another, you calculate the total you would get if you added the first number to itself a particular number of times. For example, two multiplied by three is equal to two plus two plus two, which equals six.

negative
adjective A negative number is less than zero.

numerator
noun In maths, the numerator is the top part of a fraction.

percentage
noun A fraction expressed as a number of hundredths • *The high percentage of failed marriages.*

perimeter
noun The perimeter of an area or figure is the whole of its outer edge.

perpendicular
adjective Upright, or at right angles to a horizontal line.

positive
adjective A positive number is greater than zero.

quadrilateral [kwod-ril-**lat**-ral]
noun A shape with four straight sides.

questionnaire
noun A list of questions which asks for information for a survey.

radius
noun The radius of a circle is the length of a straight line drawn from its centre to its circumference.

recurring
adjective A recurring digit is one that is repeated over and over again after the decimal point in a decimal fraction.

reflect
verb If something reflects, its direction is reversed.

regular
adjective A regular shape has equal angles and equal sides • *A regular polygon.*

rhombus
noun A shape with four equal sides and no right angles.

rotate
verb When something rotates, it turns with a circular movement • *He rotated the camera 180°.*

square
noun A shape with four equal sides and four right angles.

subtraction
noun Subtraction is subtracting one number from another, or a sum in which you do this.

symmetry
noun Something that has symmetry is symmetrical.

triangle
noun A shape with three straight sides.

vertex
noun The vertex of something such as a triangle or pyramid is the point opposite the base.

vertical
adjective Something that is vertical points straight up and forms a ninety-degree angle with the surface on which it stands.

volume
noun The amount of space something contains or occupies.

MUSIC

choir [**kwire**]
noun A group of singers, for example in a church.

chord
noun A group of three or more musical notes played together.

chromatic [kro-**ma**-tik]
adjective A chromatic scale is one which is based on an octave of 12 semitones.

composition
noun **1** The composition of a poem or piece of music is the writing of it. **2** A piece of music or writing.

crotchet
noun A crotchet is a musical note equal to two quavers or half a minim.

dynamics
plural noun Dynamics is the various degrees of loudness needed in the performance of a piece of music, or the symbols used to indicate this in written music.

harmony
noun **1** Harmony is the structure and relationship of chords in a piece of music. **2** Harmony is the pleasant combination of two or more notes played at the same time.

instrument
noun A musical instrument is an object, such as a piano or flute, played to make music.

interval

noun In music, an interval is the difference in pitch between two musical.

lyric

noun The lyric of a song is the words.

major

adjective A major key is one of the keys in which most European music is written.

melody

noun A tune.

minim

noun A musical note that has a time value equal to half a semibreve. In the United States and Canada, a minim is called a half note.

minor

adjective A minor key is one of the keys in which most European music is written.

musician

noun A person who plays a musical instrument as their job or hobby.

octave

noun The difference in pitch between the first note and the eighth note of a musical scale.

orchestra [**or**-kess-tra]

noun A large group of musicians who play musical instruments together.

percussion

noun or adjective Percussion instruments are musical instruments that you hit to produce.

pitch

noun The pitch of a sound is how high or low it is.

quaver [**kway**-ver]

noun A musical note that has the time value of an eighth of a semibreve. In the United States and Canada, a quaver is known as an eighth note.

rhythm

noun Rhythm is a regular movement or beat.

scale
noun An upward or downward sequence of musical notes.

score
noun The score of a piece of music is the written version of it.

semibreve
noun A musical note which can be divided by any power of 2 to give all other notes. In the United States and Canada, a semibreve is known as a whole note.

synchronize *or* **synchronise** [**sing**-kron-nize]
verb To synchronize two actions means to do them at the same time and speed.

syncopation
noun Syncopation in rhythm is the stressing of weak beats instead of the usual strong ones.

tempo
noun The tempo of a piece of music is its speed.

ternary
adjective Ternary form is a musical structure of three sections, the first and the second contrasting with each other and the third being a repetition of the first.

timbre [**tam**-ber]
noun The timbre of a musical instrument, voice or sound is the particular quality or characteristic it has.

triad [**try**-ad]
noun In music, a triad is a chord of three notes consisting of the tonic and the third and fifth above it.

vocal
adjective Vocal means involving the use of the human voice, especially in singing.

PE

active
adjective Full of energy.

agile
adjective Able to move quickly and easily • *He is as agile as a cat.*

athlete
noun Someone who is good at sport and takes part in sporting events.

athletic
adjective **1** Strong, healthy, and good at sports. **2** Involving athletes or athletics • *I lost two years of my athletic career because of injury.*

biceps
noun The large muscle on your upper arms.

exercise
noun **1** Exercise is any activity which you do to get fit or remain healthy. **2** Exercises are also activities which you do to practise and train for a particular skill.
verb When you exercise, you do activities which help you to get fit and remain healthy.

field
noun An area of land where sports are played • *A hockey field.*
adjective In an athletics competition, the field events are the events such as the high jump and the javelin which do not take place on a running track.
verb In cricket, when you field the ball, you stop it after the batsman has hit it.

gym
noun A gymnasium.

hamstring
noun Your hamstring is a tendon behind your knee joining your thigh muscles to the bones of your lower leg.

injury
noun Hurt or damage, especially to part of a person's body or to their feelings • *The knee injury forced him to retire from the professional game.*

medicine
noun Medicine is the treatment of illness and injuries by doctors and nurses.

mobile
adjective If you are mobile, you are able to travel or move about from one place to another.

personal
adjective Personal matters relate to your feelings, relationships,

and health which you may not wish to discuss with other people.

pitch
noun An area of ground marked out for playing a game such as football.

quadriceps
noun A large muscle in four parts at the front of your thigh.

qualify
verb When you qualify, you pass the examinations or tests that you need to pass to do a particular job or to take part in a sporting event.

relay
noun A relay race or relay is a race between teams, with each team member running one part of the race.

squad
noun A small group chosen to do a particular activity • *The England football squad.*

tactic
noun Tactics are the methods you use to achieve what you want, especially to win a game.

tournament
noun A sports competition in which players who win a match play further matches, until just one person or team is left.

triceps [**try**-seps]
noun Your triceps is the large muscle at the back of your upper arm that straightens your arm.

PSHE

ability
noun The intelligence or skill needed to do something • *The ability to get on with others.*

achieve
verb If you achieve something, you successfully do it or cause it to happen.

achievement
noun Something which you succeed in doing, especially after a lot of effort.

addict
noun Someone who cannot stop taking harmful drugs.

approval
noun **1** Approval is agreement given to a plan or request • *The plan will require approval from the local authority.* **2** Approval is also admiration • *She looked at James with approval.*

approve
verb **1** If you approve of something or someone, you think that thing or person is acceptable or good. **2** If someone in a position of authority approves a plan or idea, they formally agree to it.

communication
noun Communication is the process by which people or animals exchange information.

control
verb If you control yourself, you make yourself behave calmly when you are angry or upset.

dependant
noun Someone who relies on another person for financial support.

dependency
noun Dependency is relying on someone or something to give you what you need • *Drug dependency.*

discipline
noun **1** Discipline is making people obey rules and punishing them when they break them. **2** Discipline is the ability to behave and work in a controlled way.
verb **3** If you discipline yourself, you train yourself to behave and work in an ordered way. **4** To discipline someone means to punish them.

discussion
noun A conversation or piece of writing in which a subject is considered in detail.

effort
noun Effort is the physical or mental energy needed to do something.

emotion
noun A strong feeling, such as love or fear.

emotional
adjective **1** Causing strong feelings • *An emotional appeal for*

help. **2** To do with feelings rather than your physical condition • *emotional support.* **3** Showing your feelings openly • *The child is in a very emotional state.*

encourage

verb **1** If you encourage someone, you give them courage and confidence to do something. **2** If someone or something encourages a particular activity, they support it • *The government will encourage the creation of nursery places.*

gender

noun Gender is the sex of a person or animal • *The female gender.*

generous

adjective A generous person is very willing to give money or time.

involve

verb If a situation involves someone or something, it includes them as a necessary part.

pressure

noun If you are under pressure, you have too much to do and not enough time, or someone is trying hard to persuade you to do something.

racism *or* racialism

noun Racism or racialism is the treatment of some people as inferior because of their race.

reality

noun **1** Reality is the real nature of things, rather than the way someone imagines it • *Fiction and reality were increasingly blurred.* **2** If something has become reality, it actually exists or is actually happening.

relationship

noun **1** The relationship between two people or groups is the way they feel and behave towards each other. **2** A close friendship, especially one involving romantic or sexual feelings. **3** The relationship between two things is the way in which they are connected • *The relationship between slavery and the sugar trade.*

represent

verb **1** If you represent someone, you act on their behalf • *lawyers representing relatives of the victims.* **2** If a sign or symbol represents something, it stands for it. **3** To represent something in a particular way means to describe it in that way • *The popular press tends to represent him as a hero.*

representative

noun A person chosen to act on behalf of another person or a group.

reward

noun Something you are given because you have done something good.

verb If you reward someone, you give them a reward.

sanction

verb To sanction something means to officially approve of it or allow it.

noun **1** Sanction is official approval of something. **2** A severe punishment or penalty intended to make people obey the law. **3** Sanctions are sometimes taken by countries against a country that has broken international law.

sexism

noun Sexism is discrimination against the members of one sex, usually women.

stereotype

noun A fixed image or set of characteristics that people consider to represent a particular type of person or thing • *The stereotype of the polite, industrious Japanese.*

verb If you stereotype someone, you assume they are a particular type of person and will behave in a particular way.

RE

baptism

noun A ceremony in which someone is baptized.

Bible

noun The Bible is the sacred book of the Christian religion.

Black Stone

noun The sacred stone in the Kaaba in Mecca. Muslims believe that the stone was given by God.

Buddha

proper noun The Buddha is the title of Gautama Siddhartha, a religious teacher living in the 6th century BC in India and founder of Buddhism. Buddha means 'the enlightened one'.

Buddhism
noun Buddhism is a religion, founded by the Buddha, which teaches that the way to end suffering is by overcoming your desires.

burial
noun A ceremony held when a dead person is buried.

celebrate
verb When a priest celebrates Mass, he performs the ceremonies of the Mass.

chalice [**chal**-liss]
noun A gold or silver cup used in churches to hold the Communion wine.

Christian
noun A person who believes in Jesus Christ and his teachings.
adjective **1** Relating to Christ and his teachings • *The Christian faith.* **2** Good, kind, and considerate.

commandment
noun The commandments are ten rules of behaviour that, according to the Old Testament, people should obey.

commitment
noun Commitment is a strong belief in an idea or system.

Communion
noun In Christianity, Communion is a religious service in which people share bread and wine in remembrance of the death and resurrection of Jesus Christ.

confessional
noun A small room in some churches where people confess their sins to a priest.

confirm
verb When someone is confirmed, they are formally accepted as a member of a Christian church.

disciple [dis-**sigh**-pl]
noun A follower of someone or something, especially one of the twelve men who were followers and helpers of Christ.

Eid-ul-Adha [**eed**-dool-ah-duh]
noun An annual Muslim festival marking the end of the pilgrimage to Mecca known as the hajj.

faith
noun Someone's faith is their religion.

festival
noun A day or period of religious celebration.

funeral [**fyoo**-ner-al]
noun A ceremony or religious service for the burial or cremation of a dead person.

Hindu
noun A person who believes in Hinduism, an Indian religion which has many gods and believes that people have another life on earth after death.

hymn
noun A Christian song in praise of God.

immoral
adjective If you describe someone or their behaviour as immoral, you mean that they do not fit in with most people's idea of what is right and proper.

immortality
noun Immortality is never dying. In many religions, people believe that the soul or some other essential part of a person lives forever or continues to exist in some form.

Islam [**iz**-lahm]
noun Islam is the Muslim religion, which teaches that there is only one God, Allah, and Mohammed is his prophet. The holy book of Islam is the Koran.

Israeli [iz-**rail**-ee]
adjective Belonging or relating to Israel.
noun Someone who comes from Israel.

Jesuit [**jez**-yoo-it]
noun A Jesuit is a priest who is a member of the Roman Catholic Society of Jesus, founded in the sixteenth century by Ignatius Loyola. One of the main aims of the Society is missionary work.

Jew [**joo**]
noun A person who practises the religion of Judaism, or who is of Hebrew descent.

Judaism [**joo**-day-i-zm]
noun The religion of the Jewish people. It is based on a belief in one God, and draws its laws and authority from the Old Testament.

lent
noun Lent is the period of forty days leading up to Easter, during which Christians give up something they enjoy.

marriage
noun Marriage is the act of marrying someone.

miracle
noun A wonderful and surprising event, believed to have been caused by God.

moral
noun (in plural) Morals are values based on beliefs about the correct and acceptable way to behave.

Muslim *or* **Moslem**
noun A person who believes in Islam and lives according to its rules.
adjective Relating to Islam.

parable
noun A short story which makes a moral or religious point.

pilgrim
noun A person who travels to a holy place for religious reasons.

pray
verb When someone prays, they speak to God to give thanks or to ask for help.

prejudice
noun **1** Prejudice is an unreasonable and unfair dislike or preference formed without carefully examining the facts.
2 Prejudice is also intolerance towards certain people or groups
• *racial prejudice.*

Presbyterian
noun or adjective A member of the Presbyterian Church, a Protestant church in Scotland and Northern Ireland.

priest
noun **1** A member of the clergy in some Christian Churches. **2** In many non-Christian religions, a priest is a man who has special duties in the place where people worship.

prophet
noun A person who predicts what will happen in the future

religious
adjective Someone who is religious has a strong belief in a god or gods.

shrine
  noun A place of worship associated with a sacred person or object.

sign
  noun When talking about religion, a sign is an event or happening that some people believe God has sent as a warning or instruction to an individual or to people in general.

Sikh [seek]
  noun A person who believes in Sikhism, an Indian religion which separated from Hinduism in the sixteenth century and which teaches that there is only one God.

special
  adjective **1** Something special is more important or better than other things of its kind. **2** Special describes someone who is officially appointed, or something that is needed for a particular purpose • *Karen actually had to get special permission to go there.* **3** Special also describes something that belongs or relates to only one particular person, group, or place • *The special needs of the chronically sick.*

spirit
  noun The spirit of a dead person is a nonphysical part that is believed to remain alive after death.

spiritual
  adjective **1** To do with people's thoughts and beliefs, rather than their bodies and physical surroundings. **2** To do with people's religious beliefs • *spiritual guidance.*

symbol
  noun A shape, design, or idea that is used to represent something • *The fish has long been a symbol of Christianity.*

synagogue [sin-a-gog]
  noun A building where Jewish people meet for worship and religious instruction.

temple
  noun A building used for the worship of a god in various religions • *A Buddhist temple.*

wedding
  noun A marriage ceremony.

worship
  verb If you worship a god, you show your love and respect by praying or singing hymns.

SCIENCE

absorb
verb If something absorbs liquid or gas, it soaks it up.

acid
noun A chemical liquid with a pH value of less than 7 that turns litmus paper red. Strong acids can damage skin, cloth, and metal.

alkali [**al**-kal-eye]
noun A chemical substance with a pH value of more than 7 that turns litmus paper blue.

amphibian
noun A creature that lives partly on land and partly in water, for example a frog or a newt.

apparatus
noun The apparatus for a particular task is the equipment used for it.

chemical
noun Chemicals are substances manufactured by chemistry.
adjective Involved in chemistry or using chemicals • *Chemical weapons.*

circulate
verb When something circulates or when you circulate it, it moves easily around an area • *An open position where the air can circulate freely.*

combustion
noun Combustion is the act of burning something or the process of burning.

condensation
noun Condensation is a coating of tiny drops formed on a surface by steam or vapour.

cycle
verb A single complete series of movements or events in an electrical, electronic, mechanical, or organic process.

digestion
noun **1** Digestion is the process of digesting food. **2** Your digestion is your ability to digest food • *Camomile tea aids poor digestion.*

element
noun In chemistry, an element is a substance that is made up of only one type of atom.

evaporate
verb **1** When a liquid evaporates, it gradually becomes less and less because it has changed from a liquid into a gas. **2** If a substance has been evaporated, all the liquid has been taken out so that it is dry or concentrated.

freeze
verb When a liquid freezes, it becomes solid because it is very cold.

frequency
noun The frequency of a sound or radio wave is the rate at which it vibrates.

friction
noun The force that stops things from moving freely when they rub against each other.

gravity
noun Gravity is the force that makes things fall when you drop them.

growth
noun **1** Growth is the process by which something develops to its full size. **2** An abnormal lump that grows inside or on a person, animal, or plant.

haemorrhage [**hem**-er-rij]
noun A haemorrhage is serious bleeding especially inside a person's body.

hazard
noun A substance, object or action which could be dangerous to you.

insect
noun A small creature with six legs, and usually wings.

laboratory
noun A place where scientific experiments are carried out.

liquid
noun Any substance which is not a solid or a gas, and which can be poured.

mammal
noun Animals that give birth to live babies and feed their young with milk from the mother's body are called mammals. Human beings, dogs, and whales are all mammals.

method
noun A way that an experiment or test is carried out • *Describe the method as well as the result obtained.*

nutrient
noun Nutrients are substances that help plants or animals to grow
• *The nutrients in the soil.*

organism
noun Any living animal, plant, fungus, or bacterium.

oxygen
noun Oxygen is a chemical element in the form of a colourless
gas that makes up about 21% of the world's atmosphere. With an
extremely small number of exceptions, living things need oxygen
to live.

particle
noun A basic unit of matter, such as an atom, molecule or
electron.

predator [pred-dat-tor]
noun An animal that kills and eats other animals.

pressure
noun Pressure is the force that is produced by pushing on
something.

reproduce
verb When living things reproduce, they produce more of their
own kind • *Bacteria reproduce by splitting into two.*

respiration
noun Your respiration is your breathing.

respire
verb To respire is to breathe.

solution
noun A liquid in which a solid substance has been dissolved.

temperature
noun The temperature of something is how hot or cold it is.

thermometer
noun An instrument for measuring the temperature of a room or
a person's body.

vertebrate
noun Vertebrates are any creatures which have a backbone.

vessel
noun A thin tube along which liquids such as blood or sap move in
animals and plants.

GLOSSARY

acronym

noun A word made up of the initial letters of a phrase. An example of an acronym is 'BAFTA', which stands for 'British Academy of Film and Television Arts'.

adjective

noun A word that adds to the description given by a noun. For example, in 'They live in a large white Georgian house', 'large', 'white', and 'Georgian' are all adjectives.

affix

noun In grammar, an affix is a prefix or suffix added to a word.

alliteration

noun The use of several words together which all begin with the same sound, for example 'around the ragged rock the ragged rascal ran'.

base word

noun Same as **root word**

blend

noun A word formed by joining together the beginning and the end of two other words; for example, 'brunch' is a blend of 'breakfast' and 'lunch'.

closed syllable

noun A syllable where the vowel is followed by a consonant, for example 'cap'.

consonant

noun A sound such as 'p' or 'm' which you make by stopping the air flowing freely through your mouth.

consonant blend
noun Where two or more consonants run into each other or blend. For example, 'blanket' or 'stripe'.

etymology
noun Etymology is the study of the origin and changes of form in words.

homonym
noun Homonyms are words which are pronounced or spelled in the same way but which have different meanings.

homophone
noun Homophones are words with different meanings that are pronounced in the same way but are spelled differently.

linguistics
noun Linguistics is the study of language and how it works.

mnemonic
noun A word or rhyme that helps you to remember things such as scientific facts or spelling rules.

noun
noun A word that refers to a person, thing, or idea.

open syllable
noun A syllable where the vowel is not followed by a consonant, for example 'he'.

pronunciation
noun The way a word is usually said.

prefix
noun A letter or group of letters added to the beginning of a word to make a new word.

rhyme
verb If two words rhyme, they have a similar sound • *Sally rhymes with valley.*

root word

noun A word from which other words can be made by adding a suffix or a prefix. For example, *clearly* and *unclear* can be made from *clear*.

sequence

noun The sequence in which things are arranged is the order in which things are arranged.

strategy

noun A plan for achieving something.

stress

noun Stress is emphasis put on a word or part of a word, making it slightly louder.

suffix

noun A letter or group of letters which is added to the end of a word to form a new word.

syllable

noun A part of a word that contains a single vowel sound and is pronounced as a unit. For example 'book' has one syllable and 'reading' has two.

syntax

noun The syntax of a language is its grammatical rules and the way its words are arranged.

verb

noun A word that expresses actions and states, for example 'be', 'become', 'take', and 'run'.

vowel

noun A sound made without your tongue touching the roof of your mouth or your teeth, or one of the letters *a, e, i, o, u,* which represent such sounds.